PATTERNS IN INDUSTRIAL BUYING BEHAVIOR

PATTERNS IN INDUSTRIAL BUYING BEHAVIOR

WESLEY J. JOHNSTON

PRAEGER

PRAEGER SPECIAL STUDIES • PRAEGER SCIENTIFIC

658.72
J73

Library of Congress Cataloging in Publication Data

Johnston, Wesley J.
   Patterns in industrial buying behavior.

   Bibliography: p.
   1. Industrial procurement. I. Title.
HD39.5.J63   658.7′2   81-10745
ISBN: 0-03-059426-X   AACR2

Published in 1981 by Praeger Publishers
CBS Educational and Professional Publishing
A Division of CBS, Inc.
521 Fifth Avenue, New York, New York 10175 U.S.A.

© 1981 by Praeger Publishers

123456789 145 987654321

Printed in the United States of America

To MSJ

Foreword by

RICHARD P. BAGOZZI

Contributions to knowledge generally take one of two forms. In the first, termed normal science by Thomas S. Kuhn (1970), contributions are measured by the additions made to an existing body of knowledge. Normal science typically encompasses a refinement in, or an extension of, a recognized theory, method, or finding. The vast majority of contributions in marketing, or in the behavioral and natural sciences for that matter, is of the normal variety. Occasionally, contributions arise that address and solve long-standing anomalies, that is, problems that earlier approaches either failed to address or else found intractable. These latter contributions have been termed scientific revolutions by Kuhn to stress that they have an impact on the scientific community and its benefactors of an order more radical and important than found in the day-to-day discoveries of normal science.

Professor Johnston's research represents a contribution in this sense, for it heralds a paradigm shift within the marketing subfield of industrial-buying behavior. Indeed, his work marks one of the earliest and most extensive attempts to view industrial buying as a social phenomenon. Previous efforts have tended to limit inquiry to the study of the behavior of single purchasers, a loose description of the external constraints faced by these purchasers, or a categorization of the set of decision makers and their functions. Industrial buying, however, most often involves social processes of give-and-take, power, and even conflict. To focus only on the actors is to miss the dynamics of how decisions are actually made in response to interpersonal, group, and social structural forces.

In this book, Professor Johnston presents a new framework for viewing industrial buying. His conceptualization of the phenomenon to be explained departs from earlier perspectives in that special effort is devoted to the processes within the firm central to industrial buying. Four dimensions are identified in this regard: vertical hierarchy involvement in the buying network, lateral involvement of divisions and departments, extension or task differentiation in the buying network, and the degree of connectivity or integrative complexity in the network. The four dimensions of industrial buying are then modeled as functions of three classes of determinants: organizational-structural variables (size, complexity, formalization, and centralization), purchase-situation variables, and individual characteristics of purchasing managers (experience, specialization, and achievement). Overall, the model and findings provide an important picture of industrial buying that nicely complements the earlier pioneering work of Sheth, Webster, Wind, and others.

Marketing scholars and practitioners will find the book useful in a variety of ways. Some will use the literature review as a critical survey of the state of the art. Others will discover that the methodology opens new ways for exploring industrial buying, particularly the use of sociometric techniques for studying communication patterns. Still others will value the overall conceptual scheme provided by Professor Johnston, for it not only provides a comprehensive way to view industrial buying but it introduces new concepts and ways to model the social processes and systemic aspects of the phenomenon as well. Finally, the results of Professor Johnston's study make an important contribution to our knowledge of the industrial-buying process. He has shown us that buying is a complex sociological and psychological phenomenon that nevertheless lends itself to exploration and discovery. Professor Johnston's book is, in short, a rare piece of scholarship and will certainly have a significant impact on the field.

PREFACE

This study defined and operationalized four dimensions of the popular "buying-center" concept (members of the buying organization who interact during the buying-decision process). The four dimensions were (1) vertical involvement—how many various levels of the organizational hierarchy exert influence in the buying-decision process; (2) lateral involvement—how many different departments and divisions exert influence in the purchase decision; (3) connectedness or integrative complexity—the amount of interconnection between members of the buying center; and (4) extension or task differentiation—the total number of individuals involved in the buying-decision process. The centrality of the purchasing manager in the buying-center communication process was also examined using sociometric techniques. This provided an objective measure of the purchasing manager's influence in the communication network.

The predictor variables were concerned with structural aspects of the firm and purchase-situation attributes. The structural aspects of the firm examined size, formalization, centralization of authority, and complexity. The purchase-situation attributes measured the importance, novelty, and complexity of the purchase decision to the buying firm.

The sample consisted of 31 firms in which the purchase of an item of capital equipment and an industrial service were examined in "snowball" sampling. In all, 241 interviews were conducted. Using these interviews, the communication network for each purchase situation was constructed. The tasks each individual was involved in were also determined.

The results of the study are reported in four sections. First, sample statistics concerning the 62 purchase situations and 31 firms as well as some descriptive correlations are reported. The next section contains a regression analysis of the dimensions of the buying center against the structural variables of the firm, the purchase-situation attributes, and the characteristics of the purchasing managers involved in each purchase decision. The third section aggregates the communication networks for each product class. This aggregation presents a unique and valuable manner in which to examine industrial-buying behavior. The diagonal cells of the aggregate communication matrix depict participation on a percentage basis, while the off-diagonal cells indicate dyad formation between the various participants (who communicates with whom). The final section provides a qualitative description of the flow of the industrial buying-decision process.

The past literature has offered numerous models depicting the process as a straightforward chronological flow of easily identifiable steps or phases. The results of this study tend to refute this and indicate that while certain tasks tend to be required in most purchase decisions, the process is more iterative and tends to have no clearly identifiable sequence. A task-involvement matrix depicts the extent to which the various functions become involved in the different tasks of the buying process.

The findings also indicate that although there are differences in buying-center composition for purchases of capital equipment and industrial services, the differences are subtle and generalizations may be inappropriate. Structural variables of the firm and purchase-situation attributes were found to affect buying-center dimensions in consistent ways.

Implications of the results suggest industrial buying behavior can benefit from a more appropriate social level of analysis. The dyadic-systems approach adopted in this study presents the first significant findings concerning buying-center composition.

CONTENTS

LIST OF TABLES

LIST OF FIGURES

PATTERNS IN
INDUSTRIAL BUYING
BEHAVIOR

1

INTRODUCTION:
THE SOCIAL NATURE OF
INDUSTRIAL BUYING BEHAVIOR

PURPOSE OF THE STUDY

The purpose of this research was to develop and test an improved conceptualization of industrial buying behavior, one that drew concepts and permitted methodologies developed in the organizational behavior and social science areas. For the purposes of this study, industrial buying behavior was defined by Bonoma, Zaltman, and Johnston (1977) in the following manner:

> an explicit or implicit transactional decision making interaction through which formal or informal profit centers represented by authorized delegates
>
> (1) establish the need for products or services,
> (2) search among and identify potential suppliers,
> (3) evaluate the marketing mix (product, price, promotion, distribution) of potential suppliers,
> (4) negotiate for and enter agreement about purchase terms,
> (5) complete a purchase,
> (6) evaluate the purchase's utility in facilitating organizational goals. [P. 4]

Industrial buying behavior is the process through which industrial organizations obtain the goods and services necessary as inputs to the continuation of their ongoing processes and ultimately their survival.

Central to this view of the industrial buying process is the transactional and interactive nature of industrial buying; that is, industrial buying is not an act that someone commits but, rather, the outcome

1

of an interaction between at least two parties. In this interaction, the buyers (and others in the buying firm) and potential sellers share the interdependency of outcomes, the possibility of divergent goals and conflict, and often attempt to influence each other. Therefore, it would be more appropriate to view industrial buying as a transaction between a number of individuals rather than an action of one person called the buyer.

This definition also explicitly recognizes that there may be quite a number of intrafirm and interfirm relationships in the buying process that may not include the formally authorized representatives through which the purchasing function is carried out.

Understanding the behavior of industrial organizations as buyers is of prime importance to any complete theory of marketing. As the marketing concept (Kotler 1980) dictates, effective marketing strategies rely upon a knowledge and understanding of the buyer. This knowledge must be extended to the industrial areas if industrial marketing efforts are to be well planned and successful. In recent years, an increase in the recognized importance of industrial organizations as consumers has developed. Several recent literature reviews (Bonoma, Zaltman, and Johnston 1977; Thomas and Wind 1977) have noted a substantial number of scholarly journal articles, books, and other references concerning industrial marketing and purchasing. One researcher (Zaltman 1975), however, notes that the popular belief exists that there is not a substantial amount of research or knowledge concerning industrial-buying behavior. What appears to be the case is that the existing literature has made little impact in terms of either general understanding or specific practices.

Examination of previous research in industrial buying behavior reveals that the most basic questions are not answered, perhaps primarily due to conceptual ambiguities and methodological weaknesses. In general, the existing research in the industrial marketing area is of uneven quality and utility (Zaltman 1975). What research does exist seems to indicate that many people are often involved in influencing the buying decision of an industrial organization. Webster and Wind (1972b) developed the now widely used concept of the buying center, which views the buying process of an industrial organization as being accomplished by a number of people within the firm playing different roles (for example, decider, buyer, influencer). Not all individuals within an industrial organization become involved in every buying decision, but every individual is involved in some of the buying decisions at least as a user of the goods and services the organization buys. Empirical research has demonstrated great variations with regard to participation in buying decisions within industrial organizations (Scientific American 1969) but has not yet examined the underlying dimensions determining this variance in participation.

Robinson, Faris, and Wind (1967) have shown that purchasing decision making in industrial organizations is best thought of as a process that evolves over time. They divided this time into phases. Different situational and product characteristics were shown to affect the existence and duration of these phases in the purchasing process. Other research (Rijcke 1978; Gronhaug 1976), however, indicates that these phases are often not sequential and a great deal of looping back exists in more complicated purchase situations.

Zaltman and Bonoma (1977) have pointed out, however, that the number of unresolved questions are still numerous. The most critical of these from a marketer's point of view are, Who participates in which phases of the industrial-purchasing process? What is the degree of influence of each participant on the purchasing process? and Under what conditions do various participants exert their influence?

This study examines these questions and provides answers of an empirical nature. Specifically, this study first reconceptualized industrial-buying behavior making use of dyadic and systems concepts in order to provide an improved research approach. This approach leaned heavily upon the definition of industrial-buying behavior previously presented. Second, under this new conceptualization a methodology developed in the behavioral sciences of social psychology and sociology was applied in order to advance the state of the art concerning operationalization and measurement of the multiperson phenomena of the buying process. This methodology, referred to as network analysis of organizational communication, uses sociometric data analyzed by using matrix algebra procedures. Network analysis represents a change from "the usual monadic analysis (focusing on individuals) toward a relational type of analysis" (Rogers and Rogers 1976). This approach more appropriately fits the transactional definition of industrial buying behavior and is more consistent with a systems approach to be discussed more fully later. Four dimensions of the buying center (lateral involvement, vertical involvement, connectedness, and extension) were operationalized and empirically examined.

As Wind (1978) and Choffray and Lilien (1976) have pointed out, the area of industrial buying needs better measurement tools and methods of analysis, especially those that incorporate the multiperson nature or buying-center concept of organizations.

To better understand industrial buying behavior, marketing researchers must be exposed to the concepts and findings of the sociology of complex organizations. As Zaltman (1975) has noted, "The study of industrial marketing is basically the study of the behavior of formal organizations" (p. 8).

THE NATURE OF INDUSTRIAL BUYING BEHAVIOR

The Buying Organization as a General System

A <u>system</u> is conceived of as a set of interdependent parts (von Bertalanffy 1968). The parts or subsystems are connected by inter-relational communication. An organization readily lends itself to study or conceptualization as a system. The systems approach to concept-ualizing and studying an organization begins with the viewpoint that an organization is composed of a series of definite subsystems or functions. An organization, when viewed as a system, has some de-gree of structure and is differentiated from the environment by a boundary. An open-systems view of an organization sees the organi-zation as exchanging information and other inputs and outputs with its environment.

If one adopts this open-systems concept of organizations, three important and basic functions become apparent: input, throughput or process, and output. The industrial organization is viewed as com-posed of elements interdependently interacting with a number of other elements within the overall environment. The flow of inputs is the basic starting point in the description of an organization. In simplest terms, the organization takes resources and information (its inputs) from the larger system (its environment) which includes other organ-izations, processes these inputs (throughput), and returns them in some different or changed way (its output) to the environment and other organizations and individuals. See Figure 1.1 for a diagram of the organizational-systems concept.

Industrial Buying Behavior and the Input Subsystem

All formal organizations, such as industrial businesses, must purchase goods and services to be used as inputs into their ongoing organizational processes; without inputs into the organizational sys-tem there could not be a continued output upon which the organization depends for its survival. The industrial-business organization sur-vives as long as it can perform the functions of input, throughput, and output and its output or product is purchased in the market in quanti-ties and prices favorable to the continuation of the cycle. In this re-spect, both buying and selling are key subsystems. They provide the very necessary interfaces with the organization's environment. Buy-ing and selling roles have been referred to as boundary-spanning po-sitions. That is, they span the organization's boundary, interacting with individuals, functions, and other subsystems both internal and external to the buying organization. This study is primarily concerned with the input-subsystem process and the buying of goods and services.

FIGURE 1.1

The Industrial Manufacturing Organization as a System

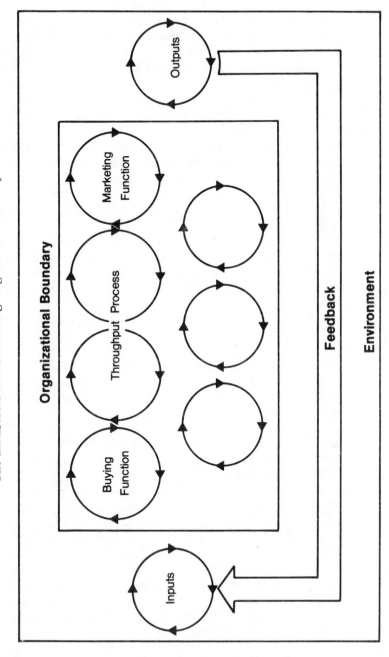

5

However, the input process cannot be separated from the through-put or output processes under a systems approach. Nor can the buying function in one firm be separated from the selling function in other firms. So, this discussion will concentrate on the interrelationships between industrial buying behavior and the other functions or subsystems in the buying firm and the industrial marketing of the selling firm.

As an example of how the buying, production, and selling sub-systems are interdependent within the industrial organization, the fact exists that purchases of goods and services by the typical industrial organization require more than half the sales revenue generated by the production and sales of the company's own goods and services. Because these purchases constitute more than half of the revenues of a firm, they are important to the efficiency of the firm from a profit perspective and require managerial decision-making emphasis within the buying firm. Every purchase, of course, is also a sale. Industrial marketers, then, must also feel it important that they understand industrial buying behavior because the marketing concept requires a knowledge of the buyer.

In large organizations, purchasing usually becomes a specialized function. But even in this situation, purchasing is not an end in itself, and the purchasing specialists need to coordinate their actions closely with the other functions and activities in the organization. A common managerial view of the purchasing function was expressed by the president of Texas Instruments in an article in Purchasing Magazine.

> We look to our purchasing departments to support our engineering efforts with ideas and suggestions and liaison with vendors, to support our marketing effort by pointing out new business opportunities and suggesting marketing approaches (not reciprocity) which can be helpful. We expect our purchasing departments, because they are in the position to be so well informed, to be a source of innovations in their own operations within the company.
>
> There is a tendency on the part of many to think that the purchasing mission is to buy things, whereas I think the purchasing mission is to be part of a larger system creating profits and growth. [Shepherd 1968, p. 61]

The interdependency of the purchasing department with other departments and functions in the industrial buying process seems obvious, yet the majority of industrial buying behavior has concentrated solely on the purchasing manager or purchasing department.

The Environment of Industrial Buying Behavior

Industrial organizations are considered a major type of firm in the producer segment of the overall economic environment. There are over 14 million different units in this segment of the economy, and each is a market for specific types of goods and services as inputs to their organizational system. These organizations employ 87 million workers, generate an output to their environment (referred to as annual national income) of $1 trillion, and comprise the marketing environment for most other firms (Kotler 1980).

The volume of interindustry sales transactions has been increasing. This indicates the increasing economic complexity of industrial technology. These transactions, excluded in the accounting procedures that determine the gross national product (GNP), have been increasing as a percentage of the GNP. It is estimated that soon the volume of industrial buying will equal the GNP (Scientific American 1969).

More dollars are involved in sales to industrial buyers than to the end market of individual consumers. It is easy to comprehend the importance of the industrial markets because of their incredible size and vast pervasiveness. Table 1.1 illustrates the size and growth of the industrial market from the perspective of several different indicators.

TABLE 1.1

Indicators of the Size of the Industrial Market:
Annual Summary, 1976-80

	1976	1977	1978	1979	1980
New Plant and Equipment Expenditures, All Industries, Total (Billion $)	120.49	198.1	231.24	270.5	294.3
Manufacturers' Orders New (Net), Total (Billion $)	1,189.6	1,354.1	1,541.9	1,732.0	1,945.9
Manufacturing Inventories, Book Value, End of Year, Unadjusted Total (Billion $)	170.4	180.1	198.0	227.7	242.0

Note: Some figures are based on preliminary data.

Source: U.S., Bureau of Statistics, Survey of Current Business, 1976-80.

INDUSTRIAL BUYING BEHAVIOR VIEWPOINTS

Industrial buying behavior has been examined from a number of viewpoints that will be discussed in detail in Chapter 2. A brief description of certain approaches and their concomitant weaknesses must be presented here, however, to support the direction of this research project.

The factors that affect industrial buying behavior have, in the past, often been viewed as economic. Economic factors were seen as having to do with cost/profit considerations. This view saw the challenge in industrial marketing as comprehending the economics of the purchasing decision as the prospective buyer saw it, understanding how the organizational rules and procedures facilitated rational decision making, and determining what motivated the ultimate choice. Account strategies, it was assumed, could be designed using certain marketing strategies that considered the differences between each potential customer.

It was also assumed, however, that whatever the size or the nature of their operations, industrial customers were in business to make a profit and, therefore, the primary buying motives were economic. These economic motives were seen as relating to price, availability of supply, and service.

Prices were simultaneously seen as being relative to the situation; that is, price comparisons were felt to be made along with other factors. The potential buyer supposedly evaluated a price quoted to the firm by comparing it with other competing offers. If the purchase was of new material, capital equipment, or a service, it was believed the buyer sought to relate the price to potential operating savings or to profits from the increased sales of the buying company's product that could result.

Availability of supply was also felt to be of critical concern to the industrial buyer. This was especially true if the product was a direct input, such as material or component parts, for the buyer's own product. Any interruption of the smooth flow of supply might foreseeably force the buying firm to shut down the production process and thereby suffer opportunity costs of lost sales and possibly customer goodwill.

It was felt that certain services added value to the basic product and were therefore important to the industrial customer. All other things being equal (for example, prices), it was felt that the marketer who offered the greatest services with his product would be the one to get the sale.

These aspects of the economic viewpoint have some merit, but because industrial buying is accomplished by people within the framework of an organization, a completely rational economic picture of

industrial buying behavior misses the point. The following generalizations help point out the human aspect of industrial buying behavior
and the subsequent effects on demand.

> (1) Price is often not the major determinant of demand,
> as buyers would be willing to pay more if certainty of
> delivery, quality, service, technical assistance, and so
> forth, were assured; to pay less for goods and be uncer-
> tain of their delivery or quality could result in huge losses
> in production delays overshadowing any savings in cost
> reductions; (2) buyers will often split purchases of prod-
> ucts rather than buy from a single source of supply; they
> do this to assure themselves of always having at least
> one source of reliable supply and to pit one supplier
> against another to obtain the best deal; (3) many buyers
> prefer to purchase from those firms they perceive to hold
> positions of technical leadership in their own industries
> with the logic that this allows the buying firm to keep up-
> to-date with technological innovations in the supplier in-
> dustry; and (4) instances of reverse elasticity of demand
> often occur in the short run owing to buyer expectations.
> [Haas 1976, p. 30]

The main point in this illustration is that people are involved
in industrial buying, and they determine or influence the final decision. A totally rational model of industrial buying behavior is insufficient in many respects. In order to understand industrial buying behavior, the interaction and interdependency of all those individuals involved in the purchasing process must be considered. The
question of just who is the industrial buyer is probably the most important and should be the first the industrial marketer asks.

WHO IS THE INDUSTRIAL BUYER?

Who is involved in the buying of the inputs needed by industrial
organizations? If viewed from the organizational level, buying organizations vary tremendously, from small firms with perhaps no full-
time purchasing specialists to huge corporations with large, centralized purchasing departments often headed by a policy-level executive
such as a vice-president or materials manager. Who makes certain
decisions or exerts influence also varies by firm. In some cases the
entire decision is made by the purchasing department; sometimes the
decision-making process is a joint effort; and in other cases the purchasing department is not involved in the decision but simply places

the order and files the paperwork. Purchasing management's authority varies among industries, organizations, and for different product categories and purchase situations. The purchasing department may make the decisions regarding less important, more routine purchases with little informational input from other functions, but the influence of others in the firm may be the deciding factor in the purchase of major capital items.

In fact, to understand industrial buying, it is important to realize that different roles may be played in buying situations. In each situation, the roles of initiator, influencer, decider, buyer, and user can be filled by different people in the buying company. For instance, in simple purchases only the user, the buyer, and the seller may be involved. In more complex or important purchases, there may be several influencers, and the final decision may have to be a concensus of opinion of all parties involved. In the most important of purchasing decisions, many members of the firm may be involved, from the board of directors and the president on down.

Thus, an important fact about much of industrial buying is that often several persons participate in or influence the purchasing-decision process. The number of persons and extent of buying influences varies with each situation and organization. Little is known, however, about the underlying dimensions along which this participation and influence varies.

DETERMINING WHO THE INDUSTRIAL BUYER IS

An Intuitive Approach

Given a reasonable knowledge of how formal industrial organizations operate, would it be possible to simply develop an intuitive approach to deciding who participates in industrial buying decisions? The answer to this question can be found in the current approaches and marketing-communication strategies of industrial marketers. In an empirical study of industrial advertisers and their customers in four industrial markets, McAleer (1974b) found that industrial marketers traditionally developed their strategy primarily on the basis of historic assumptions about industrial buyer behavior. He examined various appeals and their effects on consulting engineers, architects, and other buying-process influencers apart from purchasing agents. He found that advertisers in each of these markets did not know who the buying influencers were and therefore did not correctly perceive the effect of the advertising appeals on the respective market segment concerned. Advertising the cost savings of a product to a

production engineer who is interested in the quality and reliability of
the equipment is ineffective. In the same light, having the purchasing manager contacted by the technical sales representative in order
to influence the purchasing manager to select a particular supplier
when that decision is made by the vice-president of production is also
ineffective.

In addition, it has been estimated that industrial salesmen generally contact only one or two persons in a buying organization. What
is more discouraging, the sales representative generally misconceives
who is important in the buying organization. Functional responsibilities and job titles are not perfectly matched. A study of industrial
buying practices concluded the following.

> Suppliers have significant misconceptions about who in
> their customers' companies initiates purchases, selects
> a supplier "pool" and actually approves the final supplier.
> The role of middle management in these three functions is
> underestimated, particularly in regard to initiation and
> conclusion of a purchase, while the importance of top man-
> agement and the purchasing department is correspondingly
> inflated. ["Finding the Industrial Buying Influence" 1968,
> p. 15]

So the challenge to the industrial marketer cannot be met by making an intuitive assessment of the buying organization, its influences,
what motives and perspectives each has, and the procedures then determining the most effective way to reach them and present an attrac-
tive proposal. Empirical research is necessary to determine who
participates in the industrial buying process and what influence they
exert. The dimensions along which the influence of different functions
varies can be developed for the industrial marketer through careful research into the organizational decision-making process with respect
to industrial buying behavior.

An Empirical Approach

The challenge to the marketing researcher is to identify those
individuals within the organization who have either formal or informal
influence and authority in industrial buying decisions, for they must
be persuaded as part of the marketing task. The problem is to define
the locus and dimensions of buying responsibility within the customer
organization, define the membership of the situational buying center,
and understand the structure of authority and communication within
the buying center.

It is essential to observe people (alone and in groups), their
activities, and the communication that takes place among them in or-

der to understand the wide variety of organizational buying processes that exist and the underlying dimensions of participation in the buying-decision process. This is probably the area of industrial buying behavior about which the least is known. This is perhaps because too much of the past research tended to make two simplifications: (1) it personified the industrial buying process by postulating that the purchase decision is made by one person—the industrial buyer—or (2) it collapsed the entire process into an anthropomorphic abstraction—the "purchasing department decides." These two simplifications have led to the failure to learn anything specific about how people and departments interact.

However, in 1969 the research department of Scientific American conducted a survey of 6,000 of their subscribers (Scientific American 1969). The respondents identified themselves as holding decision-making positions in a broad range of industries and in functions fully representative of contemporary industrial management. A large number of charts and tables were compiled with information furnished about the organization of the purchasing process in the respondents' companies. It was impossible to check for converging viewpoints within specific organizations and most of the data was displayed in a statistical (bar graph) manner.

The study shows in a very aggregate way how responsibility and authority for decision making are allocated among the principal members of the management team. Significant differences were noted in the allocation of responsibilities depending upon the type of purchase and the industry of the buying firm. The ascending importance of technical considerations was reflected by the commanding role assigned to engineering and research personnel at almost every step. In the early stages of the purchase-decision process, especially when decisions turn on the writing of specifications (the fixing of standards and determinations as to the kind of material, part, or equipment to be purchased), the more technical members of the buying center appeared to emerge as the decision makers. Since early decisions tend to narrow the range of discretion at later steps in the purchasing process, this has important implications for the industrial marketer's choice of strategy.

While the Scientific American study was the important first step in pointing out that industrial buying behavior involved numerous lateral and vertical influences in buying organizations, it can be criticized on several important points.

1. Certain important underlying dimensions were not examined. Specifically, organizational-structural variables such as size, formalization, complexity, and centralization were not included in the study for their effect on functional involvement in the buying process. Pur-

chase-specific variables such as the unfamiliarity of the organization with making that type of purchase, the importance of the purchase to the organization, and the difficulty in evaluating the available alternatives were also not included as predictor variables of involvement in industrial buying behavior.

2. Only statistical averages of participation for an entire product class were developed out of the data. The involvement of individual functions over the entire sample was analyzed, but a firm-by-firm analysis was not attempted. Nor were vertical or lateral involvement examined in any systematic way other than the statistical bar graph presentation.

3. Some problems with bias and sample responses also present a problem. Specifically, more than one respondent from a firm could have been included in the study, but given the methodology it was impossible to check for a convergent picture of the buying process in each firm. This is an issue that will be covered in much greater depth later.

Certain fundamental aspects of industrial buying behavior were pointed out by this study, however. The basic need for a very detailed, case-by-case examination was identified. This type of study should analyze industrial buying organizations in terms of characteristics that would have an effect on buying behavior in specific situations, namely organizational-structural variables and purchase-situation attributes. This research would involve studying each buying organization with regard to the purchasing process and attempting to find underlying dimensions that determine involvement in the process. While it is generally conceded that the first step in understanding the very complex area of industrial buying behavior is to understand the organization of the particular firm involved and how it affects buying in specific situations, this step has not been taken in any aggregate sort of way.

This, then, was the goal of the study—to carefully examine by case analysis enough firms in specific purchase situations to be able to draw conclusions on the effect of underlying predictor variables on involvement in industrial buying. It was necessary to develop a methodology for examining involvement in the buying decision. Past research can be criticized for a number of methodological weaknesses and did not provide a methodology suitable for this type of undertaking. Chapter 2 goes into greater depth on this issue.

OUTLINE OF THE RESEARCH PROJECT

The purpose of this study was to determine the effect of organizational-structural variables and product-purchase attributes upon participation in the industrial buying decision. The reason this study was needed was that there is a lack of both descriptive evidence of what transpires in organizations relating to how purchases are made and a methodology to accurately measure the amount of influence each decision maker or member of the buying center exerts upon the others involved. In specific, the study addressed the following questions:

1. Does an organization's size, complexity, formalization, and centralization have an effect on the number of people and functions involved in the purchase-decision-making process?

2. Does a purchase's novelty, complexity, importance, and product class have an effect on the number of people and functions involved in the purchase-decision-making process?

3. What factors influence the amount of formal written communication in a purchase decision versus the amount of spoken, word-of-mouth type of communication?

4. How does the centrality of the purchasing manager in the buying-center communication network vary with organizational characteristics and purchase attributes?

5. What affects the overall connectivity of the buying-center communication network?

Chapter 2 provides a review of the state of the art of various approaches to understanding industrial buying behavior and, in particular, to participation in the buying-decision process. Emphasis was placed on identifying empirical and theoretical works relevant to this study. The purpose of this chapter was to provide the background and historical support for this study.

Chapter 3 presents a reconceptualization of industrial buying behavior. It looks at the set of assumptions the previous literature has operated under and proposes a new approach.

Chapter 4 covers the methodology of this study. It provides a review of sociometric techniques and the rationale for the particular methodology utilized, the benefits and shortcomings of this methodology, and the characteristics of the sample population. It also discusses the methods of data collection and introduces the means of analysis that were utilized.

Chapter 5 presents the research findings relating to the date collected and the analysis. Particular attention is paid to answering the questions relating to industrial buying behavior and decision participation.

The final chapter, Chapter 6, addresses the issue of the contribution of this study to the field of business administration, and what the major implications are, and provides some suggestions for future research.

2

PREVIOUS APPROACHES TO UNDERSTANDING INDUSTRIAL BUYING BEHAVIOR: A STATE-OF-THE-ART REVIEW

This chapter reviews past empirical and conceptual work in the area of industrial buying behavior. Traditionally accepted dimensions of industrial buying behavior are examined and analyzed regarding their potential for the continued advancement of the field. Previous approaches to knowledge and understanding are compared and contrasted along four major paths that run throughout most of the past contributions and can serve as connecting links in summarizing a reasonably large body of literature. The five major points around which this literature review is organized are (1) the evolution of industrial buying; (2) the sorts and types of models that have been constructed and used to characterize the industrial buying process; (3) the unit of analysis that researchers have undertaken to study, that is, what levels of aggregation (the individual, individuals, the firm, and the like) have been examined; (4) the steps, stages, or phases in the buying process; and (5) the assumptions ordinarily found in the study of industrial buying behavior.

THE EVOLUTION OF INDUSTRIAL BUYING

Prior to the 1940s and the shortage economy situations brought on by World War II (Risley 1972), purchasing was little organized and not thought to be important except perhaps in the largest organizations. Purchasing was mainly a clerical position in support of the manufacturing departments/divisions within a firm. The clerks had little expertise or specialized training other than that gathered while working on the job. Executives and production managers made most of the decisions and the purchasing clerk processed the paperwork.

According to Hill, Alexander, and Cross (1975), things began to change with the subsequent material shortages of World War II. The simple task of buying raw materials and other production goods and services became more than just a search for the lowest-priced vendor. It became a complex search for who had or would have materials and whether they could be obtained at all. The specialized position of purchasing agent began to emerge in companies with as few as 20 employees.

Other events occurring after World War II helped the purchasing agent hold on to his newly gained status. The Korean conflict often threatened new shortages or offered quick opportunities to those organizations with rapid response capabilities. The advent of the computer and its ability to quickly and accurately process stored and new information inputs aided the manufacturing and purchasing processes in organizations.

The latest stage in the evolution of industrial buying is the materials-management concept. Under this concept the various functions of manufacturing, purchasing, traffic, and inventory control are aggregated and coordinated with support from computer-information systems. In some firms a vice-president-of-materials-management position exists with requisite powers. The fact that in most industrial manufacturing organizations over half of the sales revenue goes back into goods-and-services purchases by the organization has not escaped the attention of company management.

Under this concept the industrial buying function attempts to satisfy the firm's stipulated needs (with regard to the to-be-purchased product or service) at a net satisfaction to the firm, balancing off relations with suppliers, various other functions within the organization, the desires of top management, product specifications, trade regulations, the reputation for good buying practices, price, and other commercial aspects in a complex way that defies easy modeling.

MODELS OF INDUSTRIAL BUYING

Generic Types of Models

The areas of economics, psychology, marketing, purchasing, and organizational theory have provided numerous conceptual approaches to the modeling of industrial buying behavior. There are three generic types or classes of models depicted by Webster and Wind (1972b) and used in attempting to explain the industrial buying process: task models, nontask models, and complex or joint models.

Organizational-buying behavior models can be categorized as "task" or "nontask" models. Task models are those emphasizing task-related variables (such as price) whereas the nontask models include models that attempt to explain organizational-buying behavior based on a set of variables (such as the buyer's motives) which do not have a direct bearing on the specific problem to be solved by the buying task, although they may be important determinants of the final purchasing decision. [P. 12]

Complex models are those that try to incorporate both task and nontask variables into their attempt to explain industrial buying behavior.

Task-Oriented Models

Task-oriented models tend to concentrate on the economic aspects of industrial buying. The simplest of all models of industrial buying behavior is the minimum-price model developed by economists. This model explains the behavior of firms rather than the individuals within each firm. In the case of basic commodities and other relatively undifferentiated products, the firm is believed to simply buy the product with the lowest price. This model comes out of the microeconomic literature and requires several somewhat unrealistic views of the buyer-seller relationship. These assumed views are perfect information about all competing sellers and perfect competition within the market.

A somewhat more sophisticated variation of the minimum-price model is the lowest-total-cost model. A goal of profit maximization and a perfectly informed buyer are also assumptions of this model. Other costs, however, not included in the minimum-price model are factors here. Product quality, length of life, and service requirements are examples of these costs. The buyer supposedly knows or can accurately estimate the total-cost picture for each available alternative and then chooses the one with the lowest cost.

Both the lowest-total cost and the minimum-price models rely upon an economic or "rational-man" model. Perhaps this view is better suited to analyzing how firms might optimize their buying if they could meet the strict assumptional qualifications. Subsequent research, however, has shown that these approaches are far removed from what actually does happen.

Reciprocity is another approach to explaining industrial buying behavior from a task-oriented perspective (Ammer 1962; Moyer 1970; Wind 1970). While reciprocity of an unforced nature is still legal as long as it does not restrict interstate commerce and may explain minor variances in purchasing, this variable cannot be relied upon as a sole explanatory model.

One-variable, economic-oriented task models cannot be used to reliably explain the many complexities of industrial buying behavior. Perhaps the most glaring omission of task models is the human element, for as Webster and Wind (1972) point out: "Organizational behavior is, after all, the behavior of individuals in an organizational context" (p. 88). Only the individual can have motives, emotions, cognitions, and behavior.

Nontask-Oriented Models

Nontask-oriented models attempt to explain industrial buying behavior by concentrating on the human aspects of the individuals within the firm involved in the purchasing process. Self-aggrandizement and ego enhancement are but two of the human elements thought to affect the behavior of industrial buyers. Little direct evidence of the impact of these psychoanalytically oriented task variables on the buying process exists, although it could be argued that in Strauss's (1962) anecdotal account of the lateral tactics of purchasing managers, those tactics could inherently be a result of such emotional factors.

The perceived-risk model, however, does qualify for serious consideration as an explanatory model of industrial buying behavior. This concept first originated in the consumer-behavior literature (Bauer 1960; Cox 1967) and hypothesizes that buyers perceive risk in purchase situations and act to reduce it. Levitt (1967) found high-risk and low-risk situations had important effects on the willingness of purchasing agents to make certain reported decisions. Reaction to perceived risk is believed to be higher among newer purchasing agents and becomes less accentuated as they become more secure in their jobs.

Another nontask approach to industrial buying concentrates solely on the diffusion and adoption of new products. The diffusion-of-innovations model is quite heavily researched and well formalized in both consumer and industrial buying. The research in this area has concentrated on three aspects of new industrial products' adoption by buyers: (1) identification of organizational, environmental, cultural, and legal factors that determine the rate of adoption of the innovation; (2) individual characteristics of the people involved in the buying process, which determine a willingness or resistance to adopt the product or service; and (3) the characteristics of the product or service itself that determine how rapidly and by whom a product is adopted (Zaltman, Duncan, and Holbek 1973; Peters and Venkatesan 1973). The diffusion-of-innovations model views buying behavior as the reaction to an innovation after exposure to information that the product or service is available. Resistance to innovation and length of time from either exposure to the knowledge of the product or from the market introduction are important considerations of the model. One flaw in this nontask model is that it concentrates on new products only.

Complex or Joint Models

Complex models attempt to combine a number of both task and nontask variables into an interactive framework aimed at prediction of buying behavior. A number of models can be identified as complex: the dyadic paradigm (Bonoma, Bagozzi, and Zaltman 1978), organizational interaction (Hakansson and Ostberg 1955), information processing (Howard and Morgenroth 1968), the decision-stage model (Saleh et al. 1971), competence/activity (COMPACT) (Robinson and Stidsen 1967), simulation models (Wind and Robinson 1968), the BUYGRID (Robinson, Faris, and Wind 1967), the organizational buying model (Webster and Wind 1972a), the industrial buyer-behavior model (Sheth 1973), and the industrial-market-response model (Choffray and Lilien 1978). Most of the complex models view industrial buying as an intricate process of decision making involving communication between a number of organizational members and other organizations taking place over time.

While complex models have advanced state-of-the-art industrial buying and contributed to improving research attempts, each has its flaws. Four of the best known complex models are the Robinson, Faris, and Wind BUYGRID (1967), the Webster and Wind organizational buying model (1972a), the Sheth industrial buying behavior model (1973), and the Choffray and Lilien industrial-market-response model (1978). These models are considered by many to present well-developed, comprehensive approaches to industrial buying.

Specific Models

The BUYGRID

The BUYGRID model was developed by Robinson, Faris, and Wind (1967) in a descriptive study of three organizations and a large number of purchasing situations actually faced by them. An eight-stage model of the buying process was combined with Faris's(1967) three types of purchase situations—the new task, the modified rebuy, and the straight rebuy. These three types of purchase situations were defined on three different dimensions: (1) the newness of the purchasing problem, (2) the amount and kind of information required, and (3) the extent to which new alternatives were considered. A new-task situation was one in which the organization had no previous purchasing experience, sought a great deal of various kinds of information, and considered a relatively large number of alternatives. The modified-rebuy situation occurs when the need or desire to replace an existing product or service arises. If new information and alternatives are considered along with the product or service currently in use and the experience from previous similar purchases, it is considered to be a modified-rebuy situation. The situation is not completely new to the firm, but there may be new information or alternatives to be considered. In a straight-rebuy situation, a large amount of previous purchasing experience is available and the firm simply reorders from the last supplier. No new alternatives are considered.

A problem with this purchase typology is that it seems to confound at least three separate dimensions of the purchase situation. The importance of the purchase, the novelty of the product or service to the organization, and the complexity or difficulty of evaluating the purchase alternatives all seem to be factored together. This has some undesirable properties for attempted explanatory purposes. For instance, if a company is contemplating the purchase of minor supplies not bought before (new task), such as pencils, the BUYGRID would predict a relatively more drawn-out process than a purchase by the same company replacing its old fleet of automobiles.

The model also identifies eight stages or phases in industrial buying behavior whose existence and duration depend upon the purchase situation. When a purchase is a new task, all the phases supposedly exist and are extensive. When the situation is a straight rebuy, the firm supposedly passes quickly through the phases, perhaps even skipping some. The eight phases are described as the following:

(1) Anticipation or Recognition of a Problem (Need) and a General Solution
(2) Determination of Characteristics and Quantity of Needed Item
(3) Description of Characteristics and Quantity of Needed Item
(4) Search for and Qualification of Potential Sources
(5) Acquisition and Analysis of Proposals
(6) Evaluation of Proposals and Selection of Supplier(s)
(7) Selection of an Order Routine
(8) Performance Feedback and Evaluation [Robinson, Faris, and Wind 1967, p. 14]

While this model is empirically based, it would seem to be an almost impossible task for an industrial marketer to identify those of his actual and potential customers that fall into each of the three buying situations, except through a detailed analysis on an individual basis. Different marketing strategies would be difficult to develop based only upon the use of the BUYGRID. Additional criticism of the model is found in the fact that "it is virtually devoid of predictive ability, and offers little insight into the nature of the complex interplay between task and nontask variables" (Webster and Wind 1972b, pp. 24-25). In spite of these drawbacks, the model has gained wide acceptance and is commonly used in marketing-strategy discussions.

The Organizational-Buying-Behavior Model

The organizational-buying-behavior model developed by Webster and Wind (1972a) was an attempt to integrate a large number of individual, interpersonal, interorganizational, and environmental variables into a consistent framework. The basic assertion of this model is that all organizations—profit, nonprofit, public, and private—buy in a similar manner. Organizational buying is seen as a decision-making process carried out by individuals in interaction with others in the context of a formal organization.

The organization is influenced by a number of factors in its environment including economic, political, legal, cultural, and social institutions and forces. The model emphasizes the importance of these environmental forces as determinants of buying behavior. The environment is seen as both a source of information and as a source of constraint acting on organizational-purchasing behavior.

The organization itself is also a source of influence on the buying-behavior process. Members of the buying center (defined as the set of all individuals and groups who participate in the purchase-decision-making process) are motivated and directed by organizational goals and constrained by the financial, technological, and human resources of the firm.

The third source of variation in the model is the network of interpersonal relationships among organizational members and more specifically those within the buying center. These individuals often have different responsibilities and may play different roles. Identification of each individual's role set, characterized by expectations, actual behavior, and relationships with others, is required to understand the nature of participation in the buying-decision process.

Finally, Webster and Wind see organizational buying behavior as reducible to individual behavior. The individual is at the center of the buying process. These organizational members are the targets of the industrial marketer's strategy, or should be—not the abstract entity of the organization. The model fails to establish how to identify the organizational members who play the various roles in the buying center yet emphasizes the need to understand the psychological characteristics of the buying-center members, to study their attitudes and preferences toward particular products and suppliers, and to comprehend the nature of their individual-decision processes. The model is loosely constructed and offers no testable propositions.

Although the stimulus-response framework allows excellent retro-spective explanation of purchasing decisions, at best the model provides only vague predictions of behavior. Webster and Wind note that, in their view, the model "does not claim to know what is the exact buying decision-making process . . . [but] it presents the major sets of variables . . . that marketing personnel should identify in their attempt to understnad buying behavior" (1972, p. 39).

The Industrial Buyer Behavior Model

The industrial buyer behavior model developed by Sheth (1973) is an extremely complex stimulus-response model of the buying process. A large number of variables are interwoven in a flow-chart-type diagram. The model's complexity is a result of the number of variables and the relationships between them. This is an attempt to describe and explain every type of industrial-buying decision from simple to complex. The model recognizes the existence of differences between the various members of the buying organization as to their expectations concerning product characteristics and suppliers. Empirical research on buying policies and practices of purchasing agents; observations of industrial buyers; and theories, models, and reports on industrial-buying activities are incorporated into the model in an attempt to capture the realism and complexities of organizational-buying behavior.

The industrial buyer behavior model goes a long way in reconciling and connecting many disparate pieces of empirical and conceptual work. It considers product-specific, company-specific, and individual-difference variables. Differences between individual roles are considered. At the center of the model are individuals involved in the buying process. Considerable interaction is assumed to take place between these individuals, and they are often required to decide which alternative to select jointly. Sheth feels that individuals who have different responsibilities in the organization tend to consider different criteria in their evaluation of available alternatives. It would seem essential, however, for research to first discover who has what influence under what conditions before studying their particular preference patterns.

The second part of Sheth's model concentrates on the conditions that precipitate joint decision making among the individuals involved in the decision process. The model distinguishes several factors that are either product specific, such as the repetitive character of purchase, or company specific, such as its size and managerial philosophy.

Finally, the model characterizes the process of joint decision making in industrial buying behavior. Various interparty conflict types and methods of resolution are proposed. While Sheth's model represents an attempt to apply some of the more important concepts from the area of organizational behavior to the study of industrial buying behavior, its loosely connected and vaguely defined variables produce no testable hypotheses. It does, however, enable one to begin to order the mass of existing literature and complexity of industrial marketing. In addition, recent research (Lambert, Dornoff, and Kernan 1977) has shown that parts of the Sheth model are simplistic in the treatment of cause-and-effect factors in industrial buying behavior. A revision to the model's postchoice evaluation process has already been suggested.

The Industrial-Market-Response Model

The industrial-market-response model is the most recently developed model and the first complex model to be empirically capable of validation. The major components of Choffray and Lilien's model are broken down into controllable variables, the decision process, and external measures. Controllable variables consist of the marketing support given to the product or service to be marketed and its design characteristics. In the decision process, four submodels are developed to closely follow Choffray and Lilien's conceptualization of the organizational-purchasing process. The four submodels depict awareness, acceptance, individual evaluation, and the group-decision process. External measures of concern in this model are the communication consumption for each participant in the purchasing process, environmental constraints, organizational requirements, individual perceptions and evaluation criteria, and group-process variables. This model is an attempt to parsimoniously construct a model of industrial-buying behavior that could be useful to management in constructing marketing strategy. In addition, it attempts to operationalize the concept of the buying center.

Unfortunately, the model is built upon a highly questionable assumption and a methodological flaw in data collection. Choffray and Lilien (1978, p. 22) assume that "decision participants who belong to the same category share the same set of product evaluation criteria and the same information sources." This assumption allows for no individual differences with respect to individuals in the same or similar functional role within the target organizations. A purchasing manager is a purchasing manager, and an engineer is an engineer. As will be noted later, individual motives vary quite extensively even within the same functional roles, and individual goals change over time. The assumption that information sources are the same is not correct either, although a greater similarity exists for like-category participants. The methodological flaw in the data collection lies in the Decision Matrix questionnaire. This is a crosstabulation of functional role (for example, production and maintenance engineers, plant or factory manager) by phase in the decision process. This matrix is given to individuals identified as having been involved in the purchase process, and they are asked to fill in each cell with a percentage of involvement for participant by phase. Previous research by Weigand (1966), Brand (1972), Grashof and Thomas (1976), and Rijcke (1978) has shown that each buying-center member or decision participant exaggerates his/her own importance in the process, has only a partial picture of the entire process, and does not agree with other members as to the amount of others' influence or participation.

The industrial-market-response model does have certain credits. Mainly, it recognizes the need to operationalize the buying center and develop some sort of group-measurement model. For too long industrial-buying behavior has relied on only individuals involved in the process; the unit of analysis has been strictly that of individuals. It is to this problem that we now turn.

THE UNIT OF ANALYSIS IN INDUSTRIAL BUYING BEHAVIOR

A problem to date in the study of industrial buying has been the unit of analysis. Since most of the purchasing situations encountered by organizations involve more than a single individual, it is necessary to understand the functioning of the multiperson process from a group perspective. Yet most of the empirical and conceptual studies ignore this requirement and with few exceptions (which will be noted here) focus on the individual (primarily the purchasing agent) as the sole unit of analysis. This section reviews the various levels of aggregation that have been adopted in the study of industrial-buying behavior.

The Firm as the Unit of Analysis

Because microeconomics was first used to study industrial buying behavior, a number of studies simply use the firm as the unit of analysis and disregard the individuals involved in the process. This view concentrates mainly upon the choices made and tends to neglect any process that might be involved.

In a study of industrial innovation and the diffusion and adoption of new industrial products, Baker (1975) examined the influence of organizational structure on the willingness of firms to innovate. He found that the size of a firm was the most important factor in early adoption and that increases in the size of a firm are generally accompanied by

1. An increase in the resources devoted to the acquisition and evaluation of information.
2. An increase in the resources devoted to the search for new and better ways of exploiting the firm's resources.
3. An increase in its dependence on formalized procedures and standard practices to govern its day-to-day activity, to measure its performance, and to enable it to select between alternative courses of action. [P. 137]

The plans that companies develop also can have an effect on buying behavior over both the short- and long-term planning cycles, according to Howard (1963a). These plans presumably influence the company's rate of purchases. Short-term plans deal with production and inventory levels, while long-term plans deal with plant expansion and other capital outlays. In theory, over the short term a company decides upon two quantities at the beginning of a planning period: how much to produce and how much to hold in inventory. Constraints taken into account in the development of the plan include production costs, inventory-holding costs, output limitations (plant capacity), and inventory-storage limitations. The attempted realization of the plan, Howard feels, is significant in explaining buying behavior. The long-term planning process involving capital outlays for plant and equipment typically requires a lengthier planning analysis of the future, but the planning framework is essentially the same. Factors taken under consideration in long-term plans are anticipations of future business fluctuations, plant capacity, production level, future technological changes, and future prices. There are both expansionary capital outlays to increase productivity and nonexpansionary ones for replacement and modernization reasons.

A taxonomy of product-dependent (for profit) and product-independent (nonprofit) companies was developed by Gronhaug (1976) and used for classifying organizations and comparing their buying behavior. Purchasing activities were found to be more structured in product-dependent organizations. Another important discovery was in the differences in buying motives between the two types of companies. Internal need for the purchase was more often a reason for buying by product-dependent organizations. Product-independent organizations were found to buy because money was available in their organizational budget. There was no significant difference between the two types of organizations concerning the purchase of goods and services because of innovation or adoption of new products. These results stress differences in buying behavior because of environmental influences on organizations.

In a study on the communication between firms in the steel industry concerning the adoption of an innovation, Czepiel (1974) used sociometric techniques to link firms who had communicated with each other through word-of-mouth (that is, spoken conversations of an informal nature). He found a weak correlation between the centrality of a firm in the communication network and the tendency for early adoption of the innovation.

A great deal of statistical data is available about firms and the industry they are in through the Standard Industrial Classification Manual, published by the Office of Management and the Budget, and the census, conducted by the Bureau of the Census. The Standard Industrial Classification code (SIC) is a uniform numbering system for classifying establishments in the United States according to the economic activity they engage in. The Bureau of the Census publishes statistics broken out by SIC code and county for the entire United States. The SIC code is a useful method of developing a marketing plan by segmenting organizations. In combination with the Bureau of the Census statistics, it gives a reasonably accurate picture of the geographical concentration of markets by number of firms and gross-sales revenue.

The Commerce Department's Office of Business Economics publishes a national input/output model, which is also useful on an aggregate-market basis. The concept behind the input/output analysis is the systems approach discussed in Chapter 1; that is, the sales or output of one industry are viewed as the purchases or input of other industries. Regional and local input/output models are also available. These models help to identify the current markets for an organization's goods and services in a very rough way.

Analysis at the firm or industry level is sometimes helpful to recognize trends in the marketplace or to narrow the market to which an organization should target its products but is of little or no help in understanding how to market those products. By using the firm or industry as the unit of analysis, it is possible to lose sight of the fact that people determine the size, plans, and environment of organizations. The individuals within a firm are the correct target for marketing communications and sales approaches. The first step in understanding an industrial organization is to gain as much knowledge as possible about the way people interact within that organization. The purchasing manager and the purchasing department are the most visible to outside marketing organizations. For this reason a great deal of research has concentrated on the purchasing personnel in industrial organizations. While a thorough understanding of only the purchasing manager is insufficient to be truly effective in selling to organizations, it is a reasonable starting place. The next section reviews some of the research concerned with purchasing managers.

THE PURCHASING MANAGER

The most common level of analysis in industrial buying behavior studies has been the purchasing manager. The industrial buyer is most often considered to be a single individual within the firm holding a position in the purchasing department. A large number of questionnaire and survey studies of purchasing managers have been conducted. Many of these studies were of a psychological nature and dealt with the motives, perceptions, and learning processes of the industrial buyer (purchasing manager).

Purchasing motives in the industrial buying decision process were separated into rational and nonrational (or irrational). The actions of purchasing managers were considered entirely rational or task oriented by early researchers who operated under the economic model of man previously discussed in this chapter. These rational motives, according to Hill, Alexander, and Cross (1975), were price, quality, and service from the supplier. Assurance of supply was of less importance than the others but was still considered a rational motivation of industrial buyers.

The first person to question this view of the industrial buyer appears to have been Duncan (1940). In surveying a representative sample of 400 purchasing managers, Duncan used a questionnaire that contained motives of both product and patronage types, according to his classification. Product motives concerned the actual product while patronage motives were those concerned with the seller, such as reputation, cooperativeness, and accessibility. Duncan found that while rational motives predominate, nonrational motives did have an impact on the outcome. Some of the nonrational motives Duncan detected were habit, emotional stress, caution (especially after inventory problems), and confidence of price levels. An additional finding, but one which had little effect on the study of industrial buying at that time, was that in the large majority of heavy-equipment and raw-material purchases, more than one executive influenced the decision.

More recently, Feldman and Cardozo (1969) questioned the usage of two existing views of the purchasing process they felt to be out of date. They developed their own view of purchasing from a more consumeristic approach. The first view they criticized was what they referred to as the classical or simplistic view. This is the oldest and least sophisticated view of the industrial buyer. In this view the buyer acted as a clerk, receiving requisitions from management and product information from salesmen and supplier catalogs, then matching management specifications to the lowest-priced alternative available and accomplishing the necessary paperwork. The buyer was assumed to be rational and informed. Market segmentation was accomplished along geographic, size, and product-class dimensions. Bribery of the buyer was not eliminated as a possible influencing strategy.

An extended and modified version of this basic view of the purchasing function was titled the neoclassical view. In this view the purchasing manager received more complex requisitions. He had greater discretion in purchasing and was more active. He initiated supplier contact, performed cost-and-value analysis, and attempted to minimize the firm's total cost. The objective of the purchasing manager was to obtain the best combination of price, quality, delivery, and service. An emotional element was contained in this view of the purchasing manager and brought into consideration whenever the buyer appeared to have settled for less than the best price, quality, delivery, and/or service. Advertising was considered an important tool in this approach. Feldman and Cardozo rejected this view because it was inadequate as either a descriptive model or analytical framework.

The new view of the purchasing manager suggested a consumer approach. The buyer was seen as a procurement executive. Inputs into the purchasing process came from discussions with executives in other departments and suppliers in other firms. The procurement executive was proactive rather than reactive. He initiated both intrafirm and interfirm contacts. The concepts of risk preference and resource allocation were incorporated into the purchasing manager's behavior.

Another motivating factor of purchasing managers was thought to be fear. Lazo (1960) made the statement that "fear is one of the major influences in industrial buying: fear of displeasing the boss; fear of making a wrong decision; fear of losing status; fear indeed, in extreme cases, of losing one's job" (p. 258).

While fear may perhaps be too strong a concept to consider as a motivating factor of purchasing managers, researchers have discovered a tendency toward risk reduction and a need for certainty in industrial buying. Sweeney, Mathews, and Wilson (1973) examined the relationship between industrial buyers' risk-reducing behavior and their need for cognitive clarity and cognitive styles. They found that the greater the need for cognitive clarity, the greater the risk reduction desired. Specific cognitive styles were also found to determine risk-reducing behavior. Their findings provide a way to segment purchasing managers for different marketing approaches.

Peters and Venkatesan (1973) found that perceived risk and self-confidence were related to the adoption of a small computer system. Wilson (1971) identified three decision-making styles of industrial buyers and found that an individual's need for certainty appears to be an important influence upon choice under conditions of uncertainty. In a similar study, Wilson, Mathews, and Sweeney (1971) reported results of a study of industrial buying decision making in which only the purchasing agent was responsible for the decision. They found two main patterns of industrial buying behavior and two major decision styles. The buyers were classified as behaving in a rational or nonrational manner and deciding in a normative or conservative way. The normative decision-making style selected alternatives with high expected monetary value (EMV), especially in choices where uncertainty was high and the amount at stake significant.

The perceptual process of industrial buyers has also been of interest to researchers concentrating solely on the purchasing manager. In a study on supplier selection, Hakansson and Wootz (1975) found that purchasing managers perceived price to be more important than quality. The location of a supplier was also perceived as important, especially in an international purchasing situation. This study also examined the effects of education, experience, and the environment on the purchasing manager's risk reduction. Education appeared to have the greatest effect on behavior.

Wildt and Bruno (1974) built a model to predict the preference for capital equipment using only purchasing managers. They found that a linear-compensatory model performed equally well (poorly) with or without weights.

Parket (1972; 1973) examined the effects of product perceptions on industrial buying behavior. He found that for products that were perceived as highly similar, the price, specifications, and delivery were important purchase attributes. This study of 600 industrial buyers classified products into generic (undifferentiated) and nongeneric (differentiated) categories. For generic-product classes, certain company-specific features could also help in making the sale. These included a broad product line, close geographic location, cooperation on unusual size orders, ease of placing an order, reputation, previous performance, and the particular salesman involved.

A study conducted by Lehmann and O'Shaughnessy (1974) implicitly recognized the importance of others within a firm in buying decisions but used only purchasing agents in the sample. Nineteen U.S. and U.K. firms were studied in an attempt to classify industrial products and determine choice criteria used by purchasing agents to select suppliers. Products were classified into four groups according to potential problems they might generate through their purchase.

1. Routine-order products (little or no problems),
2. Procedural-problem products (problems in learning how to use the product),
3. Performance-problem products (problems in satisfactory performance by the product), and
4. Political-problem products (problems in reaching agreement among those affected).

Information acquisition and processing by purchasing managers has also been studied under the single, individual unit of analysis. Stiles (1973) showed that industrial buyers exhibited differing levels of information processing as a function of the amount of structural complexity in the specific purchasing task, individual differences in conceptual capacity, the total work load, the quality of communication with the product users served, and the number of participants in the decision process. Monoky, Mathews, and Wilson (1975) found that information-source preferences of industrial buyers were a function of the buying situation. The buy classes (new task, modified rebuy, straight rebuy) can be thought of as differentiated by the magnitude of uncertainty associated with each situation. It is maximal in the new task and minimal in the straight rebuy. Monoky (1973), in a separate study, concluded that industrial buyers' preferences for information sources vary as a function of the amount of uncertainty in the buying situation. Buyers were found to have a marked preference for personal sources in both the new-task and modified-rebuy situations.

While it should be evident that a purchasing agent's motives and perceptions, as well as his unique method of processing information and decision making, must affect the purchasing process that takes place, it is also equally evident that the buyer is not acting alone and is actually involved in a system of inter- and intrafirm transactions and has a functional role that he must perform. Most current views of industrial buying explicitly include the influence and actions of others besides the purchasing manager.

Other Individuals within the Buying Organization

While most of the approaches to industrial buying behavior discussed in the preceding section have focused on the purchasing manager, most current views include the effects of the influence, interests, and actions of others within the firm on the purchasing managers. Weigand (1968), in his article on the insufficiency of only studying the purchasing manager, showed that the industrial buying function is substantially more complex than it initially appears. It involves many people at all levels in a firm, often with vastly differing views. Purchasing a particular product or service can often be a protracted activity. The final choice may be influenced by factors that are largely unrelated to the quality and price of the product being sold (for instance, reciprocity). The main sections of Weigand's article examined the varying use expectancies of individuals, the purchase time-span, the responsibilities of various individuals, and the existence of outside influences.

Perhaps the first article to indicate that a number of people other than purchasing personnel were involved in buying decisions came out of research conducted by Cyert, Simon, and Trow (1956). They also found that decisions in organizations varied widely with respect to the extent to which the decision-making process was programmed. Both repetitive, well-defined (programmed) decisions and highly unstructured, rather detailed (nonprogrammed) decisions were identified. The researchers believed a continuum existed along which all decisions could be classified. In addition, they commented on how actual business decision making varied from the economic model and noted the participation of various individuals enacting subroutine programs.

Buzzell's (1964) casebook contains a descriptive study noting the participation of some 14 people involved in the purchase of a $3,000 air compressor. Stevens and Grant (1975) devoted an entire book to examining the "purchasing/marketing interface." Brand (1972) conducted a study based on 232 semistructured interviews with people involved in the buying process within 43 U.K. companies. A number of different industries were represented. Each company employed over 250 persons. Brand examined the participation of key departments and individuals in the different stages of the decision-making process for new buys, modified rebuys, and routine repurchase situations. He found that general management and technical personnel were perceived as equal or more important than purchasing management in most of the stages.

The frequency of involvement of different organizational functions (for example, production, purchasing, research and development) in the purchasing-decision process has also been investigated on a number of occasions (Buckner 1967; Scientific American 1969; Choffray 1977). These studies typically involved a survey of a large cross section of industrial firms, from which aggregate frequencies of involvement were computed on an industry or product-category basis. No attempt has been made by any of these studies to group and systematically investigate the characteristics of organizations and/or products that have similar patterns of involvement in their purchasing process. Buckner (1967) noted that the purchasing decision is a joint process involving three groups of specialists (up to eight people): top management, operating management, and production engineers, for capital goods and equipment; the buying department, production engineers, and operating management, for materials and components.

Other researchers have attempted to discover what aspects of an organization and the purchase situation bring the different participants into the decision-making process. Gronhaug (1975a) examined the purchasing process of specialty stores in Bergen in an effort to determine if the occurrence of autonomous or joint-buying decisions correlated positively with the novelty of the buying problem, the pur-

chase of production goods (products and services directly related to
the end product) as opposed to institutional goods (products and services necessary to keep the organization going), size of the purchase,
and organizational size. His model of the purchase decision stated
that the type of decision (autonomous vs. joint) was a function of the
degree of routinization of the buying problem, the perceived product
importance, and the available resources for handling buying problems.
In another study by Gronhaug (1977), he found that the initiation of a
purchase for a computer was more often a function of top management
than other departments in profit-making organizations.

Robey and Johnston (1977) developed a model depicting two dimensions of participation in industrial buying decision making: lateral
and vertical. Eight hypotheses were constructed from a review of the
current literature. These hypotheses are as follows:

(1) The larger the size of an organization, the greater
its internal differentiation and the greater the extent of
lateral influence on buying decisions.

(2) The more variety in an organization's environment,
the greater its internal differentiation and the greater the
extent of lateral influence on buying decisions.

(3) The more uncertain the organization's buying environment, the more differentiated the buying function
and the greater the extent of lateral influence on buying
decisions.

(4) Size is not related to the vertical distribution of
influence on buying decisions. However, increasing size
is related to the way in which that influence is exercised.

(5) Environmental uncertainty is related to greater discretion of lower levels in buying decisions and a smaller
extent of vertical influence.

(6) The greater the scope of a purchase, the greater
the extent of lateral influence and the less the discretion
of lower levels in buying decisions.

(7) The greater the complexity of a purchase, the
greater the extent of lateral influence and the greater the
discretion of lower levels in buying decisions.

(8) The newer a purchase, the greater the extent of
lateral influence and the greater the discretion of lower
levels in buying decisions. [Pp. 454-59]

Patchen (1975), in examining the locus and basis of influence
in organizations on the purchasing decision, outlined a conceptual
approach to studying interpersonal influence. He found that data concerning the bases of influence in organizations—especially that showing

the importance of a person's stake in the decision—did not fit neatly into the well-known influence categories of French and Raven (1959). Disagreements raised questions about the general applicability of certain often-used measures of influence in organizations and the results of a series of studies examining perceptions of influence in the purchasing process. As a result, Patchen turned to a panel of judges for their opinion as to who had the most influence in the purchasing process.

Backhaus and Gunter (1976) felt that, to a certain extent, who enters the buying center was controllable by the selling organization.

> To the marketer, who is not interested in having a consulting engineer in on the decision-making process, this means taking measures to reduce the customers perceived risk which prompts him to bring in a consulting engineer. Very effective incentives in this respect are such services as providing know-how, technical assistance, favorable warranty conditions, references. [P. 269]

A number of other studies have also examined the perceptions of influence in the purchasing process and found a similar lack of agreement. Bearden (1967), in measuring the occupational status of purchasing agents, found that top management was more similar in their judgments on reciprocity, competitive bidding, restricted sales-calling hours, and back-door selling to purchasing management than to sales management. Bearden interpreted this to indicate that purchasing management's status was higher than sales management's. These results are somewhat surprising in light of the fact that top management tends to rise out of sales/marketing positions more often than out of purchasing.

Weigand (1966) collected different opinions within firms as to who was influential in the purchasing process. He found that purchasing managers tended to rate their concern with different responsibilities in the purchasing process higher than others in the firm tended to. This is an indication that purchasing management may overrate its involvement and importance in industrial buying.

Cooley, Jackson, and Ostrom (1977) analyzed the perceptions of the relative power of various functional groups in the modified-rebuy purchasing decision for industrial components. They found that perceptions of power differed significantly between the supplier-selection decision and the product-selection decision. The size of the firm, the type of product, and the type of manufacturer each affected the perceived power of the various participants. Traditional product characteristics were shown to have mixed results in affecting the power of the various functions. The dependent-variable power was measured by allowing representatives from purchasing, production, engineering, and other functions in each firm to allocate 100 points between the decision participants. The mean score of all raters was used.

Grashof and Thomas (1976) also conducted a study into the perceptions of influence over the specific stages of the decision process in a situation dealing with the purchase of scientific and technological information. Besides a wide divergence between self and others' perceptions in general, they found that the variance of the perceptions was relatively small across the several stages of the decision process.

In the most recent study to examine this subject, Rijcke (1978) found that purchasing and nonpurchasing members of the firm had divergent views about their respective roles in the purchasing process; that even multiinterviewing did not solve the problem of whom to believe or how to resolve conflicts; and that breaking the global question of influence into more specific influence areas may increase convergence between self and others' perceptions of influence over the purchasing-decision process.

The question of whom to believe when the perceived roles are different among the various members of the firm is difficult to answer. Perhaps a closer examination of role theory as it has been applied to industrial buying and how the various members involved in the purchasing-decision process interact will be helpful. Tushman (1977) examined the need for innovating systems to gather information from and transmit information to several external information areas. He found that special boundary roles evolve. These boundary roles link the informal organizational network to the external information sources. Purchasing and marketing are two such boundary-role functions.

Jackson and Sciglimpaglia (1974) viewed the purchasing-decision process as a complex interaction of intra - and interorganizational parties. "The other members of the role set communicate these expectations through formal and informal information flows, attempts to influence, and nonverbal communication, as the sent role" (p. 17). They saw the importance of recognizing the multiplicity of these influences and their situational nature in defining the buying center. Gorman (1971) also commented on the importance of the role concept in understanding purchasing behavior. There are natural conflicts between the purchasing department and other functional departments because different people see the purchasing department differently, and the sent role and the perceived role differs.

Kernan and Sommers (1966) developed a behavioral matrix to help clarify the roles of purchasing managers. They put forward an information-processing model in which institutional role commitment was matrixed against the probable way in which buyers think of their roles, expected commitments to role activities, and probable dominant buying motive. In empirical research on role differentiation in industrial-buying decisions, McMillan (1973) examined how role position differences and similarities affected vendor-selection decisions in U.S. firms. He identified the fact that occasions when the purchasing agent is not the most influential person in the decision-making process are increasing in frequency. McMillan felt industrial buying behavior is best conceptualized as a form of decision making involving several members of the firm who act collectively and could be called the buying center. He found that others besides the purchasing agent are involved in vendor selection. Sometimes members of the firm hold opposing views toward a particular vendor's offer.

Roles are determined by interaction with other persons. The concept of a purchasing role and the research conducted in this area indicates that the purchasing manager is not isolated from others within his firm. Studying the purchasing manager is not enough. To understand industrial-buying behavior, one must understand how others affect the purchasing manager's role and how the purchasing manager affects others in the buying center.

In adapting Heider's (1958) balance theory to explain actions of the buyer in group-buying decisions, Wind (1971) found different buying priorities depending upon whether the purchasing function was centralized and under corporate management or decentralized and under divisional or plant management. Duncan (1966) examined how the purchasing manager struggles for power in the organizational setting. "Purchasing officers . . . are both seekers of status and advocates of professional advancement" (p. 22). They push to improve their own performance, their department's work, and for better understanding by other department heads, according to Duncan.

Strauss (1962) conducted field interviews and administered questionnaires to 142 purchasing agents and found that the work behavior of the agents is strongly influenced by lateral negotiations. Interactions between purchasing and other departments such as engineering and scheduling cannot be understood in terms of the traditional, vertical supervisor-subordinate or line-staff concepts. Strauss also found the skillful and ambitious purchasing agent uses formal and informal techniques in order to influence the terms of the requisitions that he receives. In this manner, the purchasing agent introduces a two-way, role work flow and raises his own status.

Pettigrew (1975) saw the industrial-purchasing decision as a political process. In one case study concerning the purchase of a computer, Pettigrew examined the amount of communication coming into and going out of the buying firm. He found that certain individuals acted as "gatekeepers" within the firm's buying center. These individuals structured the outcome of the purchase decision through the control of information in order to maintain or improve their position in the political process.

Opinion leaders in firms can be identified to some extent by demographic and other variables (Martilla 1971). Informal conversation or word-of-mouth communication is important in the latter stages of the industrial-adoption process. Martilla found opinion leaders to be more heavily exposed to impersonal sources of information than other buying influentials in the firm.

While word-of-mouth seems to exist within a firm, its widespread existence between firms is questionable. Webster (1970), in interviews with industrial buyers, failed to identify a significant amount of word-of-mouth communication in industrial markets and suggested that manufacturers' sales representatives could perhaps serve this role.

Spekman and Ford (1977) found it possible to classify organizational members according to the type and degree of purchasing-related uncertainty they perceive in their roles as members of the purchasing decision-making unit. They also found that different buying-center members have different information requirements because of the differences in their required roles.

In an attempt to model buyers' product and evaluation strategies, Scott and Wright (1976) found that engineers were better able to process more information on product characteristics than purchasing managers. This was a contrived study, however, and external validity seems questionable.

The buying center is a complex, multiperson group of individuals within the buying organization. Each individual has an assigned role in the firm and may be involved in the purchasing process either formally or informally. Both practitioner and academic have commented on the complexity of this group of individuals.

> The chain of influences in most industrial buying situations is long, involved, and even mysterious. [Walsh 1961, p. 170]

> Patterns of influence within a given buying organization and among the various companies in an industry make industrial markets complex targets for marketing effort. [Webster 1968, p. 301]

> Traditionally, most approaches to understanding buying behavior have tended to focus on the individual buyer. If, however, buying decisions involve several people, the limitations of such an approach are evident. [Wind 1971, p. 206]

Do industrial marketers know how to reach and influence the various members in the buying center? An empirical study by Mc-Aleer (1974b) of advertisers and customers in four industrial markets revealed that the answer is apparently "no."

Lehman and Cardozo (1973) have done some research into the preferences of purchasing agents and managers in other functional fields in buying firms concerning product or institutional advertisements. They found it depends primarily upon the size of the selling firms, with small firms better off doing institutional advertising.

The area of interfirm communication needs more research. Industrial advertising is only one way firms communicate to potential customers. In the next section the dyadic concept is explored. This is one level higher in the unit of analysis of industrial buying behavior and makes the assumption that the smallest level of successful research must take at least two units together and examine the interdependencies between them. So far, the literature examined has dealt only with individuals, the purchasing agent, and others within the buying firm involved in the purchasing decision.

The Dyadic Paradigm

The dyadic paradigm, or view, has as its basic tenet the belief that the smallest unit of analysis should be the interaction of two individuals. The dyadic paradigm, therefore, has as its subject matter the two-person, two-group, or two-organization interaction. In industrial buying, the dyadic paradigm places the emphasis on the interactions that take place between the buyer and the seller. To study either the buyer or seller alone would violate the social nature of the buying process. At this level of analysis, personal and role-typical relationships between the buyer and seller are emphasized. The behavior of the buying and selling representatives is influenced by role expectations. These expectations are a product of the specific interaction situation. Both the buyer and seller enter each situation with prior expectations for their own and the other party's behavior. In the interaction process, the buyer affects the way the seller will behave through his reactions to the seller's efforts. The seller has his effect on the buyer through his own reaction to the buyer's motives.

The idea of studying the dyad as the basic unit of marketing was probably first put forward by Evans (1963). Evans used the dyadic-relationship model to study the interaction between insurance salesmen and their customers.

The dyadic paradigm as the unit of analysis has received a great deal of recent attention. Kiser, Rao, and Rao (1975), in a study of vendor-attribute evaluations of buying-center members, found that both buyer and seller had the most to gain when they viewed their relation as one of mutual benefit rather than as conflict. They felt the buyer had a broad range of marketing strategies available to increase his chances of consumating a transaction with the seller.

Busch and Wilson (1976) found the stronger the expert and referent power bases of the salesman, the more trustworthy he was perceived to be by the customer. Expert power was more powerful than referent power in affecting trust. The salesmen high in referent power, however, had a wider range of influence than did a low-referent salesman. When a salesman had a great amount of referent power, he was able to exert influence in a large number of situations and under differing circumstances.

Hakansson and Ostberg (1955) felt that dyadic interactions between buying and selling firms result in relationships of mutual dependence involving commitment to each other. They examined possible organizational-design strategies for restructuring the industrial-marketing firm for better interactions with customers. Their approach described the purchase transaction as a social-exchange situation between the buyers and sellers in the market. They felt this view was more accurate than the view of a one-sided relationship between an active marketer and a passive customer. Three different types of interactions were depicted by Hakansson and Ostberg; these interactions were a function of the complexity of the product being bought. They distinguished situations for the completely standardized product, the somewhat complicated product, and the complex product. With the completely standardized product, it was felt that a marketing department was not even needed.

Bagozzi (1975) saw marketing as an exchange process. He described three generic types of exchange: restricted, generalized, and complex. The industrial buyer-seller dyad and the interactions that take place would be considered restricted exchange under Bagozzi's typology. Restricted exchange, according to Bagozzi, refers to two-party reciprocal relationships in which the two parties exchange something (money, a product, services, and so on) that the other wants. Restricted exchanges supposedly exhibit two characteristics: an attempt to maintain equality, especially in repeatable social-exchange acts, and a quid pro quo notion—something of value in exchange for something of value (p. 33).

Bonoma, Bagozzi, and Zaltman (1978) examined the dyadic paradigm and used an actual purchasing agent-salesperson interaction to exhibit the strengths of this approach to understanding industrial-buying behavior. They saw the ability of this approach to substantially advance marketing knowledge.

Robertson (1971) felt communication between buyer and seller was a two-way system of interaction, especially when they were involved in close interactions such as the bargaining-and-negotiation process. It has been proposed by numerous researchers that communication is best understood when it is viewed as a transaction with both the speaker and the audience being active participants.

The buyer-seller dyad is an important part of the total picture of the interorganizational-influence process, but it is not the entire picture, as will be argued in the next section.

The Systems Model

As was argued in Chapter 1, probably the best way to incorporate and understand all of the complexities and interactions that take place in industrial buying behavior is a systems approach.

Zaltman and Bonoma (1977) noted that a major research problem in industrial-buying behavior was the measurement of the phenomena. They felt it was beyond dispute that buying decisions were a function not only of the purchasing representative in each firm but of all the interactions that occur in the environment, between the firms, and within each firm.

> Analyzing the individual in interaction with other persons
> while most meaningful is very difficult methodologically
> compared to the much less meaningful approach of just
> studying the individual purchasing agent. [P. 55]

They felt there was a need for new methodologies that would facilitate studying buying centers as units of analysis rather than individuals.

While a number of researchers have conceptually examined the problem (Bonoma and Johnston 1978; Cyert and MacCrimmon 1968; Cyert and March 1963; Anyon 1963; Bonoma, Zaltman, and Johnston 1978; Choffray and Lilien 1978) and others have called for work in the area (Nicosia and Wind 1977), a very limited amount of empirical work has actually been done.

Driver and Streufert (1966) outlined a model of information processing in systems of all types. Their "phasic model" of information processing postulates that at least two subsystems exist in each information-processing system. One subsystem is termed the perceptual subsystem and is largely concerned with data search and intake. This subsystem then transmits digested input to the second subsystem—the executive subsystem—which translates input into necessary decisions, actions, and strategies.

Schroder, Driver, and Streufert (1966) suggest that not all output is systematically related in input complexity. They proposed that it was only the "integrative complexity" in output that related to input complexity. In their view, information-processing systems could be described in terms of the number of parts at work (people, departments, and so on) in a system, termed differentiation, and the amount of interconnection among parts, termed integrative complexity.

Shaw (1964) identified two concepts in group patterns of communication. He suggested that the various effects of communication networks upon group behavior could be accounted for by the two concepts, which he labeled independence and saturation. Independence could also be called autonomy or self-realization and has to do with the answer-getting potential of individuals and the degree to which an individual is dependent on or under the information control of another individual. Saturation may also be labeled vulnerability or demands and has to do with the amount of information input and output an individual has to deal with. Shaw believed that performance and satisfaction in the group was a function of independence and saturation.

In marketing, only a few researchers have examined the effects of group interactions on buying behavior. In the consumer area, Arndt (1967) examined the role of product-related conversations in the diffusion of a new product. This study measured word-of-mouth among married students concerning the diffusion of a new food product. He found positive word-of-mouth had a positive effect on adoption. The degree of sociometric integration in the group was positively related to both word-of-mouth communication and adoption. In another study using housewives and consumer products, Witt and Bruce (1972) found that brand choice could be explained by group structure and the degree of symbolic involvement. However, predictor correlates were found to be situation specific.

In the industrial buying-behavior area, only a few studies that actually take a group perspective can be found. Choffray (1977) found that companies exhibited different vector involvement patterns in the purchase of industrial cooling systems. He had difficulty, however, in correlating this with any easily measurable variables. The vector involvement pattern is simply a list of departments within a firm with a binary (yes or no) scoring for participation in the decision.

Hillier (1975) studied 17 widely different organizations over a three-year period. He expressed the following:

> It seems that the existing categorization of capital equipment, raw materials, components, etc., is very production oriented, and should be reconsidered from the consumer's viewpoint, hence adopting a marketing approach.
> [P. 100]

He reclassified industrial purchases under the following taxonomy: production services, advisory services, and ancillary services; production facilities, primary equipment, operational equipment, and ancillary equipment; product constituents; and product transformers. In addition to this buyer-oriented product typology, Hillier also developed a group model of the purchasing process. This model was called the decision atom viewpoint. In the center or nucleus was the project team; the first level of electrons orbiting the nucleus was the group of individuals exerting primary constraints, then a level of relevant others, and finally a level of others outside the firm. The complexity of the decision atom was felt to be a function of the commercial complexity of the negotiations, the behavioral complexity of the human interactions, and the characteristics of the product.

As one can see, the industrial buying process has been analyzed at several levels. The greatest amount of research has been conducted at the individual level, either studying only the purchasing manager or examining the many others involved in the firm but from an individual, stimulus-response approach. The most promising research, in the opinions of many, must use dyadic levels of measurement and incorporate a group level of analysis. It is to this purpose the present study is aimed. Communication between individuals will be the measurement, and all individuals involved will be incorporated into the analysis.

The industrial buying decision has been conceptualized as a process taking place over time rather than as a simple choice process. Some researchers have felt there are a number of distinguishable stages or phases through which the decision passes in a chronological order. This area of the industrial-buying process is examined in the next section.

THE STEPS, STAGES, OR PHASES
IN THE INDUSTRIAL BUYING PROCESS

In their study of group problem solving, Bales and Strodtbeck (1951) empirically identified differentiated phases in group decision-making processes. By phases they meant "qualitatively different subperiods within a total continuous period of interaction in which a group proceeds from initiation to completion of a problem involving group decision" (p. 485). The phase hypothesis is the proposition that under these conditions groups tend to move in their interaction from a relative emphasis upon problems of orientation (giving and asking for information, clarification, and confirmation), to problems of evaluation (giving and asking for opinions, analyses, and expressions of feeling), and subsequently to problems of control (giving and asking for suggestions and directions).

Perhaps the first attempt to understand the industrial buying, decision-making process was the study of Cyert, Simon, and Trow

(1956) previously discussed. From their observations, they documented three aspects of the decision process.

1. Common processes, which are routine and recur within the organization at various stages in the decision;
2. Communication processes, which represent the information flow within the organization; and
3. Problem-solving processes, which deal with the location of viable alternatives for solving the buying problem.

Cyert, Simon, and Trow called the processes they identified program steps. They traced the program steps from inception of the problem to selection of a consultant. They also identified subprograms and contrasted the overall processes with the economic model in vogue at that time. They found the following:

1. The alternatives are not usually given but must be sought (search for alternatives).
2. The information as to what consequences are attached to which alternatives is seldom given (search for consequences).
3. Simple single criteria (for example, profit) are not used in comparisons among alternatives (evaluation).
4. The problem itself is not a given but must be identified and defined (problem definition).

Cyert, Simon, and Trow provided a useful starting point from which numerous other researchers have examined the buying process. In an attempt to model the industrial buying process, Webster (1965) identified four elements or stages in his model of how the industrial-buying mechanism operates. They were problem recognition, organizational assignment of buying responsibility, search procedures for identifying product offerings and for establishing selection criteria, and choice procedures for evaluating and selecting among alternatives. Webster's four-stage model generated interest in the concept of phases in the buying process. Two years later, Robinson, Faris, and Wind (1967) expanded the four-phase model. Their eight-stage model was previously discussed in the BUYGRID model section.

In a study of the purchase of motor carrier services (Saleh et al. 1971), four stages in the buying process were identified. The stages were problem recognition, search processes, choice procedures, and postchoice evaluations.

In the adoption of a machine-tool innovation, Ozanne and Churchill (1971) identified five dimensions of the industrial-adoption process. They were factors that set the process in motion, those that direct final purchase, the duration of the process, other alternatives considered, and the function of information sources. Their basic model had three parts: the antecedents, process, and results of the adoption process. They recognized the similarities between the industrial buying process and the adoption process they had been studying and, as a result, proposed a new, five-stage model applicable to the process involved in the buying of new products. The stages were awareness, interest, evaluation, trial, and adoption (AIETA).

McMillan (1973) also identified five stages, but they were closer to the more traditional stages previously discussed. They were recognition and definition of the problem, definition of alternatives, information search, development of decision criteria, and choice of vendor(s).

Probably the most complex model using phases to describe the industrial-buying-decision process was developed by Backhaus and Gunter (1976). Their interactive-process model depicts 12 phases, each with several dimensions, some of which occur simultaneously. The model has moved the stage or phase concept almost into a PERT, or critical-path-method, model.

Choffray (1977) in his dissertation felt that each specific product has its own unique number of stages in a purchase-process model. He developed five stages in the process of purchasing industrial cooling equipment. But if this is so, it would seem equally likely that each firm might have a different number of unique stages through which it passes because of some unique formalization of the buying-decision process or something different about the firm itself. Each specific situation could possibly consist of a different number of unique actions and interactions, and probably does. This specification of a limited number of phases through which all organizations pass in a chronological sequence begins to become suspect when the number of different research studies specifying different stages are examined. In defense, it can be argued that the specification of these stages is a useful device to aggregate all of the hundreds of actions and interactions into a manageable sequence of events. This argument, however, has been attacked by a number of researchers (Webster and Wind 1972b; Gummesson 1978; Wind 1978).

Webster and Wind (1972b) note the following:

> All buying decisions begin with the identification of need and culminate in the selection of one or more suppliers. Each of the . . . stages of the decision process is likely to occur as a more or less distinct and identifiable phenomenon, although some stages may be repeated several times and the organizational buying process may "jump around" from one stage to the next. After the vendor has been chosen, a variety of decisions may be required to

maintain and administer the buyer-seller relationship.
[P. 112]

Gummesson (1978) found that

it is essential to stress that the steps in the process are
not consecutive and clear-cut save to a limited extent.
The people involved jump rather from one step to another, backwards and forwards. The process therefore
is iterative rather than sequential. [P. 236]

In addition, Nicosia and Wind (1977) felt an organizational-decision process consists of two main components: individuals and activities.

The real payoff is to find operational ways to merge the
two approaches, for neither one alone can give . . . a
complete and useful description of organizational buying
and thus provide the basis for designing optimal buying
processes and evaluating their performance. [P. 111]

On the other hand, the literature has, unfortunately, stressed one or
the other. In summarizing their argument, Nicosia and Wind proposed that the first task was the identification of all activities at the
most basic level and all individuals involved in the process to be used
in the construction of a matrix depicting these "subject-activities."
    Other researchers have also argued for more detailed analyses
of the specific phases of the industrial buying process. Robinson
(1968) placed emphasis on problem definition and solution using conceptual frameworks and management-information-systems models.
Gronhaug (1975b) conducted research into the search process. He
developed a model in which he hypothesized that the amount of search
was a function of the perceived product-performance risk, the time
pressure for a solution, and the ability to handle new information.
He found a significant relationship for the amount of search and the
risk and information-handling ability.
    Moriarty and Galper (1978) believed product categories exhibit
wide variations along the following dimensions: the level of expendi-
ture and, therefore, the financial risk to the buying organization; the
size and structure of the decision-making unit; and the complexity and
technical content of the decision-making process. They felt that a
classification of buying categories would be useful for marketing
strategy only when considered in the context of a specific product
category. They suggested crossing the new-task, modified-rebuy,
and straight-rebuy typology with the product classes of capital equip-

ment, raw materials, industrial services, component parts, and the like.

THE ASSUMPTIONS ORDINARILY FOUND
IN THE STUDY OF INDUSTRIAL BUYING BEHAVIOR

As a way to summarize this chapter and to critique the existing research in industrial buying behavior, it is necessary to list and examine the assumptions most commonly used by researchers in this area.

It appears that a significant amount of research into the area of industrial buying has failed to make an impact on marketing thought or practice. For instance, in a recent exhaustive review of the literature (Sheth 1977) over 1,000 references were cited, yet the author of this review pointed out that the popular belief was that there is not a substantial amount of research or knowledge about industrial buying behavior. In addition, both industrial-marketing practitioners and academics are unsure of how to use current models of organizational-buying behavior for the planning of industrial-marketing activities (Choffray and Lilien 1978).

The importance placed upon studying industrial marketing seems insufficient when the relative importance of the consumer and industrial areas are compared. This tendency for marketers to overlook the importance of studying the industrial buyer is unfounded. Industrial marketing has been said to consist of those residual categories of "other markets," including producer (industrial), which although not of "prime importance" or a "major rationale for the existence of other markets," nonetheless are "large ones and challenging to the marketer" (Kotler 1976, p. 98). As these phrases indicate, industrial marketing has been considered a less immediate, exciting, or clearly delineated subject than others among the subdisciplines of marketing. Dollar comparisons, however, indicate that this lack of interest in industrial marketing is a mistake. For instance, as was noted in Chapter 1, the dollar volume involved in industrial buying far exceeds those of the consumer market, and, by 1980, it is expected that the dollar volume of the industrial market will exceed the gross national product (Scientific American 1969).

The reasons for these inconsistencies can perhaps be partially found in current methods of conceptualizing industrial-buying behavior and subsequent, inappropriate research approaches. Traditional conceptualizations of industrial buying behavior and research approaches have been characterized by a number of basic assumptions (Bonoma, Zaltman, and Johnston 1977).

The first assumption is that industrial buying behavior may be studied separately from selling behavior as actions taken by a separate individual or individuals in the firm. One of the major consequences of this assumption has been a focus on individualistic variables in the study of industrial buying behavior as they affect the industrial buying process. Thus, this separation assumption yields such constructs as individual choice processes, personality and intrapersonal dynamics, and economic models of individual expected utility and rationality. The theoretical coherence of these variables depends totally on the acceptance of the separation assumption. Using either the dyadic paradigm or a systems model of industrial buying behavior would generate a different set of constructs. The dyadic paradigm asserts that buying is an interactive process that cannot be studied in isolation from selling, and that buyer-seller dyads (two-person groups) should be the basic units of analysis for studying the transactions of the firm. The systems assumption goes one step further than the dyadic paradigm and asserts that buying behavior can only be understood as a system affected by all inputs, throughputs, outputs, actions, and interactions both within and outside of the organization.

The second assumption is that the appropriate way to approach and model industrial buying behavior is through a stimulus-response view of cause and effect. Closely related to the separation assumption is the stimulus-response view of causal inference. The industrial buying process is viewed under this model as a response generated by an individual buyer as a result of the buyer's exposure to various stimuli coming from industrial salesmen, advertising, promotions, and so on. Webster and Wind (1972b) state the following:

> A model of organizational buying behavior can take one of two forms: (1) a stimulus-response type model which relates inputs (marketing stimuli) to output (buyer's response); or (2) a stimulus-respondent-response model which consists of a set of propositions about how the buyer responds to marketing stimuli, and may provide some generalizable answers about how inputs lead to outputs. [P. 8]

This is not an accurate picture. There are other options for modeling buyer behavior besides the stimulus-response and stimulus-organism-response models. If one uses a unit of analysis such as the dyad or system, a better way to view the causal nature of industrial buying-behavior interactions would be more oriented toward a transactional viewpoint. The critical mediators between the parties to the purchase transaction would be interactive constructs such as trust, friendship, or interdependence.

The third assumption is that the key theoretical processes occurring in industrial buying behavior are rational decision making, including decision optimization; strategic choice processes; and information processing. The assumption that choice processes and prescriptive-decision-optimality indexes should be the major explanatory constructs in the industrial-buying area is consistent with the two previous assumptions. The major distinguishing characteristic between the industrial market and the consumer market is often seen as the rational emphasis placed on cost factors and economically justified decisions by the industrial buyer. There is nothing inherent in the industrial-purchase process that demands the assumption of buyer rationality or economic optimization in the industrial market. The major factors influencing the industrial-purchasing decision from a dyadic or systems perspective would be social ones, not rational economic ones. Attraction, influence, power, and reputation are factors that would develop out of a social model of the industrial buying process.

The final assumption is that the industrial buying process takes place over time and is a logical, chronological series of well-planned and executed stages of rational decision making. On the surface and for a limited number of actual purchase decisions in any firm this could be true. If one goes below the surface, however, the decision-making process is a mass of interactions involving communication between people both inside and outside the firm.

A number of studies have tried to measure influence in each of the supposed stages. These attempts have not been successful and contradictory results are usually obtained. For the studies that have ignored their own contradictory findings and attempted to specify individuals or departments with the most influence in particular stages, cross-study validation and interstudy reliability have been lacking.

Perhaps instead of prespecifying the stages of the process and then forcing all actions and interactions to be classified in one of the stages, it would be better to measure all atomistic occurrences and then build a model with these. Whether the need is suddenly realized or planned in the budget, the buy-class, formalization of the buying process, and many other factors control the flow of the decision making. These factors also need to be identified and analyzed.

THE FAILURE OF THE TRADITIONAL ASSUMPTIONS

Out of the previous traditional assumptions examined, the one that is perhaps the most inhibiting to the advancement of understanding industrial buying behavior is the assumption that the behavior of the industrial buyer can be separated from the behavior of others who make up the buyer's role set and studied in isolation. This assumption leads to the adoption of the stimulus/response model for research and to the other assumptions concerning the rationality, logic, and orderliness of the industrial buying process. This individual-level unit of analysis is the level at which most of the research to date has been collected. The single unit of analysis under the separation assumption is a problem for the following reasons (Bonoma and Johnston 1978):

1. It is reductionistic. That is, it takes a rich and complex problem and breaks it down into its component parts. It then proceeds by studying each piece in a stimulus-response (input-black box-output) manner. After having analyzed each piece, it attempts to create overall structure by piecing the entire puzzle together. Separating a transaction into reactive bits is often nonproductive and may lead to spurious conclusions.
2. By using the individual-level unit of analysis, many of the relational parts of the process are lost to descriptive explanation and management control.
3. Social behavior, by definition, is not performed in isolation by a single individual. The most important variables in social science are those of a transactional, interdependent, or relational nature.

If one accepts the study of marketing as a social science or at least as a social-problem area, then one is led away from the individual as the unit of analysis and the stimulus-response account of industrial buying. In the next chapter, a new conceptualization of industrial buying behavior will be presented. This view of industrial buying will incorporate dyadic units of interaction and be at the systems level of analysis. The model attempts to examine the many interactions that occur both within the buying firm and between the buying and selling firms.

EVALUATION OF EXISTING RESEARCH

Many of the traditional assumptions used to examine industrial buying are inappropriate for understanding the complexity of the subject (Johnston and Bonoma 1977). Most of this research has had a microanalytic orientation; that is, it concentrated on individual firms as opposed to entire industries or the total market. The objective of these studies has been to dissect and understand the decision process that led to the final purchase choice rather than accounting for the firm's final choice.

From previous speculating and limited research, it is believed that organizational buying decisions usually involve several people who have different responsibilities in the organization and who play different roles in the buying process; that the organizational-buying process can be divided into phases, and specific individuals with different job responsibilities are believed to be associated with each decision phase; and that situational aspects and product characteristics bring different participants to exert their influence in different purchasing situations.

Four models have made the most significant contributions to date in the literature. They are the Robinson, Faris, and Wind BUYGRID (1967); the Webster and Wind model (1972a), which incorporates the concept of the buying center; Sheth's (1973) model patterned after the Howard/Sheth model of consumer behavior; and the industrial-market-response model (Choffray and Lilien 1978).

A number of other empirical studies dealing with specific aspects of organizational-buying behavior have been conducted. Many one-firm case studies and single-industry analyses can be found in addition to extremely broad questionnaire surveys. The research can be grouped into three relatively homogeneous types: (1) observations of organizational-buying behavior in specific purchase situations; (2) analyses of the aggregate frequencies of involvement of different organizational functions in the purchasing process; and (3) studies of the behavior and decision style of specific, formal-role, decision participants (for example, purchasing managers, engineers).

In spite of the vast amount of research related to industrial-buying behavior, surprisingly few studies have focused on participation. The buyer's focus developed in the purchasing management literature seems to be mainly a normative approach designed for the purchasing manager with almost no emphasis of a descriptive nature. The overall impression is that the various pieces of research are scattered with relatively few attempts to further generalizations and theory building.

The literature developed in industrial buying behavior has concentrated on describing the "what" of buying decisions. Listed in a chronological and exhaustive way are the activities that are the necessary components of a buying process (for example, preparing specifications, searching for sources, vendor's evaluation, and selection). Activities, however, are not the only relevant aspect of any individual or organizational-decision process.

A more complete picture of decision making in an organization includes the observation and understanding of who performs what activities, both at the individual and group levels. The question of why certain activities are performed by certain individuals or groups in some types of firms but not in others is important. The difference in activities may be due to factors internal to the firms (for instance, differences in the formalization of the buying process, centralization/decentralization of the purchasing function, the level in the firm for which the purchase is intended, personality and group traits) and/or because of factors concerning the product (for example, the complexity of the purchase under consideration, the importance of this particular purchase to the company, and the novelty or type of purchasing situation.

Describing decision processes (that is, how people interact among themselves through formal and informal ties within an organization and across organizations) is the most important consideration not yet dealt with.

Of all the things we know about industrial-buying behavior, the thing we know the least about is who is involved. We know what is bought and how much is spent, but without a knowledge of who is exercising influence in the buying center—or for that matter, who is even involved in the buying center—it is impossible to develop communication strategies. If it can be determined who has what influence under what conditions in industrial buying behavior, personal selling and advertising can be made more effective. There are also implications for product design. Before studying the preferences of individuals within the buying firms can make sense, it must be determined who is the central person in the purchasing process and who else is involved. Once this is known, understanding their preferences becomes important.

In 1965 Purchasing Magazine (Purchasing Magazine Readers) surveyed 603 chemical-industry purchasing executives. The survey disclosed that in only 13 percent of the cases the purchasing agent alone chose the source of supply for the purchaser's products. And in 10 percent of the cases, buying influences other than the purchasing agent chose the source of supply. In the remaining 77 percent of the cases, the purchasing department and the other departments agreed upon the approved sources of supply, and then the purchasing department selected the particular supplier. The average number of influencers in the process was five.

While personal selling has been the primary promotional-mix variable in industrial marketing, the need for an efficient advertising strategy becomes clear when the industrial-buying process is seen to incorporate many individuals exerting influence at different times and on different tasks. Often these buying influences are inaccessible to the sales representative. They do, however, exert considerable influence on the buying process. Understanding who exerts what influence, under what conditions, is the first step in formulating industrial-communication strategies. If these influences can be identified, industrial marketers can design information-dissemination strategies to fulfill the role of reaching the right persons with the information needed. Once these influences have been identified, their preferences for media and product characteristics need to be identified; but that comes later.

There seems to be an almost complete agreement that purchases ought to be studied from a process perspective. This leads to the conclusion that if industrial-buying behavior within and between organizations involves many participants and is a process, then it is a social one and should lend itself to a social analysis. Recently, several approaches have been proposed that borrow from the social sciences. These studies and a reconceptualization of industrial buying behavior that is more social in nature and uses the dyadic unit of analysis will be discussed in the next chapter.

3

RECONCEPTUALIZING INDUSTRIAL BUYING BEHAVIOR: TOWARD AN IMPROVED RESEARCH APPROACH

The purpose of this chapter is to develop a new conceptualization of industrial buying behavior. Once this has been done, the conceptualization can be used to develop a model of the industrial buying behavior process and to generate a set of research hypotheses for testing.

Although, as was detailed in the preceding chapter, almost all industrial buying behavior research to date has used the individual as the unit of analysis, the reconceptualization of this phenomenon proposes that the relationship between individuals should be the unit of analysis. Thus, the dyad becomes the smallest unit of analysis, and a step toward a systems perspective, in which sociometric measures can be used, is developed.

THE NEED TO MOVE AWAY FROM THE TRADITIONAL ASSUMPTIONS

The current assumptions and research approaches examined in the previous chapter can be criticized on the grounds that they have not produced a coherent research attack on industrial buying behavior. The unit paradigm has been primarily limited to investigations of the behavior or actions of purchasing agents (or the firm taken as an anthropomorphic entity) or to the properties and characteristics of these units of analysis. Typically, studies under unit examination are individual buyers, suppliers, sales representatives, or distributors. Thus, under the current unit level of analysis such behaviors as the preferences of industrial customers, the response of middlemen to various situations, the risk reduction in purchasing highly visible products by purchasing managers, and the closing activities of sales representatives are the main focus of research investigations.

In addition, researchers have primarily relied on the classical stimulus-response (S-R) model, or variants of it, to explain the variations in the actions of those individuals or firms being examined under the single-unit paradigm of analysis. The research focus is, therefore, limited to functional relationships between observed changes in behavior of buyers and changes in the stimuli or environment impacting upon them. This individualistic S-R approach, focusing on choice processes and rationality within purchasing managers or others acting as buyers, has received wide application in research studies in industrial buying behavior. Even at the macrolevel of analysis, the industrial organization has been viewed as an entity "pushed" or "pulled" by environmental forces or stimuli (Cyert and March 1963).

Problems that can be identified as a result of the use of the single-unit-of-analysis paradigm in research on industrial buying behavior are listed by Johnston and Bonoma (1977):

(1) The unit paradigm takes a naive and unidirectional view of social causation in the industrial buying-behavior area as "moving" from stimulus to response; it is not acknowledged that responses also influence their stimuli, as in classical operant conditioning.

(2) The well-known problem of reductionism is prevalent in the unit paradigm. Forcing what is in reality a transactional phenomenon into an (atomistic) individualistic framework, and then attempting to reassemble the components is essentially futile.

(3) The most basic, and most serious problem is [that] . . . unit paradigm views [neglect] . . . the social character of industrial buying behavior. Purchases are better viewed as negotiated settlements between all those individuals involved internally in the buying firm and those external to it. These interactions lead to a purchase decision that is truly some social resultant of these interactive forces. [P. 249]

The need to move away from the traditional research assumptions has been clearly detailed by a number of researchers (Bonoma, Bagozzi, and Zaltman 1975; Bonoma, Zaltman, and Johnston 1977; Nicosia and Wind 1977).

MOVING AWAY FROM THE TRADITIONAL ASSUMPTIONS

Because the current assumptions and research approaches of industrial buying-behavior studies can be criticized on the grounds that they have not led to a coherent attack on the topic, the need exists to provide a reconceptualization of the subject before attempting new research. It is desirable that any new conceptualization of industrial buying behavior be more conducive than previous attempts to the development of explanatory mechanisms and much better suited for concerted empirical efforts. The basis of such a reconceptualization lies in a shift in the paradigm used to structure research approaches to industrial-buying behavior. The shift recommended by Johnston and Bonoma (1977)

> moves from a noninteractive, primarily individually based paradigm that takes the purchasing agent or the firm as its central focus toward a transactional, interactive, mutual interdependence paradigm taking interactions between the purchasing agent and relevant others both internal and external to the buying firm as the basic units of analysis. [P. 248]

An open-system model of industrial buying behavior can shift the nature of research in this area from an atomistic research focus on individuals as the unit of analysis to dyadic or other relational units in which communication relationships constitute the main research emphasis and to more system-level concerns involving communication-network analysis. All organizations are social systems and all social systems are communication networks held together by the flow of information (Zaltman, Duncan, and Holbek 1973).

Jacobson and Seashore (1951) proposed that the structure of an organization can be conceptualized and described in terms of the regular, work-related, interpersonal communication patterns that are extablished between pairs of individuals. From this viewpoint the organization is conceived of as a bounded social system in which a relatively stable network of interpersonal communication linkages exist. Messages that affect the productivity and maintenance of the system flow through this network taking various paths depending upon a number of variables. To some extent these dyadic links are prescribed by and reflect the formal structure of the organization.

The most important variables in a dyadic analysis are the relational variables between the two parties. While relational variables are the key constructs to the communication exchange, the dyadic approach does not exclude the use of other variables of which there is already a general understanding. Other variables that could be included in a dyadic-model analysis would be situational variables (Bonoma, Zaltman, and Johnston 1977). With a dyadic approach, however, these other variables would be primarily used to support and understand the relational variables. Situational, individual, and normative variables would not be the key constructs. The key questions to be answered in a dyadic approach, according to Bonoma and Johnston (1978), would be the following:

How and why do certain . . . interactions come about?

What are the dynamics of the relational aspects of the interaction?

What exchanges are taking place between the various dyads in the system?

What causes certain . . . relations to form and others to terminate?

How do the supporting variables (situational, individual, and normative) change with respect to the type and milieu of the interaction?

What is the effect on the interaction as the supporting variables change? [P. 217]

In collecting and analyzing data, the formal structure is disregarded and information about dyadic communications is obtained directly from network members. This information provides a record of message transactions between pairs of members. When all the communications between members are assembled, they form topological maps. These topological maps take the form of an organizational sociogram and permit locating each member at the focal point of a unique set of information vectors (Thayer 1967) or the set of previous message transactions with other members of the organization (Schwartz and Jacobson 1977). Each of these "structural maps" is unique. The communication pattern may never occur exactly like that again.

Bonoma, Bagozzi, and Zaltman (1978) argued that the dyadic approach is a fledgling systems perspective and therefore only a special case of a system. They argued, however, against moving toward a full-fledged systems perspective. Their main points against a systems approach at that time were the following:

(1) At this stage of its development, systems "theory" is primarily a descriptive tool (e.g., the flow chart) which does not admit of rigorous hypothesis formulation, testing, or theory-formation.

(2) While systems theory may in fact present a more veridical view of the marketing world than a dyadic perspective, rigorous theories and confirmed empirical relationships from social psychology and

sociology employing a dyadic perspective are more
readily available for extrapolation and extension to
the marketing discipline.

(3) A systems perspective ordinarily commits its advocates to certain generic assumptions about both system performance and/or subsystem process. [Such
assumptions may be truer in one than other systems:
for example, it is extremely dubious that individual
behavior is replicated by organizational "actions,"
pp. 57-58.]

Rogers and Rogers (1976) basically agree that system theory
has not yet had much of an impact on the study or organizations. But,
they point out the following:

The potential of open system theory in affecting the actual
research operations of communication investigations in
organizations has not yet been fulfilled, because appropriate research techniques for studying "wholes" are not
yet available. Perhaps communication network analysis
offers the greatest opportunity in this direction. [P. 118]

But, "acceptance of the systems viewpoint [implies] a concern
with studying wholes, rather than mechanistically investigating the
relationships among variables measuring some component of the individual or the organization" (p. 118), and therefore attacks the most
serious of the traditional assumptions brought to bear in the study of
industrial buying behavior. In addition, "if one accepts the notion
that all of the elements in a total system are in interdependent relationship with each other, the search for cause-and-effect relationships
is futile" (p. 118). Thus, another traditional assumption of industrial-
buying research is dispelled.

The systems model is the most appropriate model for understanding the industrial buying process. It captures more of the actual
dynamics involved in the entire complex process. Every action of
each dyadic interaction is available for examination and potential understanding. The easily measured situational and structural variables can act as supporting variables in the understanding of the relational outcomes of the industrial buying phenomenon. The major
question remains, Can a sufficiently sophisticated systems approach
to industrial buying behavior be developed?

EVOLVING NEW APPROACHES

As has been pointed out, industrial buying and marketing are
multidimensional processes. Understanding them must include not

only the activities of the buying process but also the people who initiate and perform these activities and an evaluation of the forces working on the process in specific situations. An emerging approach moving toward a systems perspective recognizes these complexities and, according to Nicosia and Wind (1976), has the following characteristics:

1. The new approach focuses on the process of organizational decisions by people leading to and following the act of purchasing. This calls for the description of a buying process over time in great detail: the interactions of people and activities (that is, who does what, when, and where) are mapped out by flow charts or digraphs (directional graphs) (compare Robinson et al. 1967; Calder 1977).

2. The approach is descriptive. The researcher simply asks, "How did the purchase evolve?" instead of asking "How should purchasing be accomplished?" This descriptive rather than normative approach must come first in the scientific examination of organizational-buying behavior.

3. Description requires observation and this, in turn, requires the choice of what and how to observe. The models and research methods to be employed are those found in behavioral sciences, primarily sociology and social psychology.

4. The notion of rationality, so prevalent in economics and early investigations of purchasing by organizations, is not given primary emphasis by the new approach. The emerging research argues that the behavior of a buyer cannot be classified as rational or irrational unless the buyer's preferences are known. Industrial buying behavior is seen to be affected by both economic, task-related variables and social/psychological, nontask-related variables (Webster and Wind 1972b).

5. Industrial buying activities involve many people who occupy a variety of buying roles. The buying process tends to be diffused throughout an industrial organization, and the persons occupying each role in a given organization are likely to change from one purchase situation to the next. The new research approach strongly argues that observation and measurement should not necessarily be concerned with the purchasing manager, but with the buying center (that is, all those individuals and groups who participate in the purchasing-decision process and who, although interested in a purchase, may have different risks arising from the decisions and, therefore, different product preferences).

6. Industrial buying behavior is a system of dynamic interactions among individuals within the context of a formal organization. Intraorganizational processes (that is, buying) and interorganizational processes (that is, how two or more organizations interact before,

during, and after a transaction) are the essentials of the industrial-buying process (Bonoma, Zaltman, and Johnston 1978).

Two approaches that have shown promise recently are those previously examined by Spekman (1977) and Calder (1977). Both researchers felt an individual level of analysis of industrial buying behavior was not very useful in capturing the dynamic interactions among those organizational members who share in the purchasing process. The buying center is a vague construct (fuzzy set) reaching across functional role boundaries whose composition can only be determined through empirical investigation.

Spekman, following a contingency-related model, conceived the buying center as a "decision unit" whose members are involved with making purchasing-related decisions. Structural properties of the buying center can be obtained by analyzing data about the relations of each buying center member to some or all of its members. In this fashion, the buying center exists as a communication network that does not necessarily derive its structural configuration from the formal organization per se, but rather from the regularized patterning of behavior and communication flows that typify the industrial buying-decision process. The buying center's structural configuration serves to define its decision-making potential.

Research on organizational-structural aspects has concentrated on five dimensions of structure: centralization (the degree to which authority, responsibility, and power are concentrated within an organization); formalization (the extent to which activity in an organization is formally defined by rules and procedures); complexity (the degree to which tasks are differentiated by a division of labor); participation in decision making (the extent to which organizational members are involved in decision making); and size (how large the organization is in comparison to other organizations). From these dimensions of structure, an organization can be positioned along several continuums. A particular organizational profile would presumably influence the particular communication network, concentration of authority, work flow, and so on among the buying-center members.

These constructs, however, may not completely reflect the pattern of informal interactions among the buying-center members. The various sociometric and informal interactions emerging during the industrial buying process, as well as the formal organizational hierarchy linkages, must be examined to give a full picture of the organizational communication network. In addition, as was previously noted, there appears to be a relatively low degree of consensus among the various buying-center members with respect to their perceptions of the buying-center structure (Spekman 1978). This makes it necessary to obtain a more accurate picture of the buying center by locating and interviewing every participant. Thus, a more relevant and potentially successful research approach would be a methodology that could focus on the purchasing process at a collective level of analysis, yet still retain the essence of individual behavior. It is to be remembered, however, that this collective is probably shaped by macro- and situation-specific factors, as well as by the individual interactions that occur (Bonoma, Bagozzi, and Zaltman 1975).

Calder (1977) has shown that role theory can provide a conceptual framework for connecting individuals together into a collectivity. Role theory is also a useful vehicle for bridging the gap between the organizational and individual levels of analysis. Using digraphs (directional graphs), Calder illustrated how in one firm the set of tasks, positions, and persons were interrelated in a structural-role analysis. This type of role-theory analysis concerns itself primarily with the structure of role relationships. Basic to the concept of role structure is the view that any group of individuals is connected by the various tasks that must be accomplished. The particular communication pattern that emerges establishes specific relationships among the members of the collectivity. Depending upon the situational aspects and organizational structure, the communication pattern will involve different group members in different task relationships.

A second element of structural-role theory, the concept of positions, connects a particular formal role to a task element. In examining the different tasks in the purchasing process, it may be discovered that a particular task is always the responsibility of a certain formal role(s). For instance, the production engineer may always be responsible for designing the product specifications, while the purchasing manager always drafts the purchase requisition and files any subsequent transmissions. In this manner, the set of interactions illustrated by the various positions within the buying center serves to establish the formal relationships among buying-center members, represent the functional role (for example, purchasing manager) assigned to a particular task, and indicate what influence each functional role exerts on the particular buying task. In other words, the concept of position defines one's location on an organizational chart and specifies the nature of one's formal interactions with other members of the organization or organizational subunit (in this case, the buying center).

Since the formal structure of an organization, in many cases, does not depict all the interactions within an organization, a third set of relationships emerges. This third set of relationships concerns the informal interrelations developed by persons who are individuals initially connected by their occupying particular interdependent positions. These relationships are not usually depicted by the formal hierarchy of the organization. It can be seen that this set of individuals serves to complete the communications network not fully accounted for by the more formal delineation of positions or tasks. Digraphs, which are patterns of relationships among pairs of abstract elements (Harary, Nouman, and Cartwright 1958), can have a system of different graphs within the overall framework.

Calder's series of graphs consisted of a P-graph depicting formal relationships among buying-center members, a T-graph detailing the sequence of purchasing-related tasks, and an H-graph outlining the informal relationships among the buying-center members. From this highly schematic digraph, the interpersonal dynamics of the buying center can be examined in minute detail. Not only can one more easily discern the sequence of purchasing-related events and the various positions sharing these activities but one can also trace the informal power relationships and other sociometric connections. The structural-role approach offers a basis for aggregating across organizations while still preserving an individual-level perspective. However, the structural-role-analysis methodology is presently not well developed, but it is a useful conceptual framework for capturing the microlevel relationships that lie at the core of the buying-center construct. Structural-role analysis, then, is not a method in and of itself; it merely provides a guide by which to conduct collective-level analyses.

These two new approaches, the macrosociological method and structural-role analysis, contain promising conceptual designs and the final steps toward really meaningful research analyses for understanding the process of organizational-buying behavior. It seems that an approach that combines the best of both of these would take further strides in enabling researchers to understand organizational-buying behavior and the functioning of the buying center.

For instance, if digraph analysis were used to construct communication networks depicting the purchase decision in a number of firms buying different classes of products (capital equipment, industrial services, and so on), then these digraphs could be examined for similarities varying across firms and product-purchase situations. That is, if the buying-center networks were developed, certain matrix algebra concepts of graph theory could be borrowed from the social sciences (for example, social psychology and sociology) to develop dependent measures of these interrelationships. Patterns of involvement in the buying center such as centrality, connectedness, and subgroup formation are probably affected by structural variables of the specific organization and the particular product class being purchased. Secondary characteristics of the product such as its novelty to the particular firm, complexity, and overall importance in relation to other purchases made by the firm can be hypothesized to also affect the buying-center membership and functioning.

The remainder of this chapter details these considerations and presents a model specifically developed in a dyadic-systems context using dyadic interactions as the basic unit of analysis in an attempt at a better understanding of organizational-buying behavior. It should be pointed out that this model is not a totally complete, general-systems-theory model. A model of that level would include all levels of coalition formations starting with the dyad and moving through triads, tetriads, and so on to even larger size groups of interacting individuals. The final section extracts testable hypotheses for empirical examination.

A MODEL OF COMMUNICATION NETWORKS AND INFLUENCE PATTERNS IN INDUSTRIAL BUYING BEHAVIOR

Theory

A major assumption of this research undertaking is that industrial buying behavior is best described with reference to multiple organizational roles serving different functions related to buying decisions. The buying-center concept views the actual locus of decisions in the purchasing process to be a fuzzy set, where individuals exert influence and are participants under some circumstances, but this varies; formal job titles (for example, finance officer, purchasing manager) may provide clues but no definitive answers to the question of who exerts what influence under what conditions or circumstances. Identification of these sources of influence is, of course, fundamental to the study of industrial buying behavior. Once location of influence, or where and how decisions are made, has been determined, further research may be fruitfully directed at examining the decision processes of participants, the bargaining modes among departments, and the tactics of affected parties. An understanding of organization structure is a necessary complement to the analysis process. The dimensions of industrial buying behavior addressed in this research will be the involvement of the buying-center participants, the centrality of the purchasing manager, and the overall connectivity of the group interaction. These measures are primarily concerned with the location of influence and the degree of interaction within the buying center and only secondarily concerned with the interpersonal process.

The Model

Diagraming the communication network and influence patterns in the industrial buying center is important to understanding the purchasing process and designing marketing strategies for industrial organizations. An efficient and effective marketing strategy should be aimed at the specific individuals within the firm having authority and responsibility for buying decisions and not at some broad, vague entity of the organization (Webster and Wind 1972). The individuals that participate in the buying process (the buying center) make the industrial-purchasing decisions and not the organization. Research with unstructured groups has shown that the most central individual is usually viewed as the leader and has the most influence. It can be hypothesized that the same is true for the industrial buying center, which is often an informal, unstructured group. While the purchasing manager is officially responsible for the buying activities of a firm, research has shown that others are often viewed as more influential in the activities involved (Weigand 1966). Therefore, by measuring the centrality of the purchasing manager in the buying-center communication network, we obtain a surrogate for the overall power and influence of that individual. In addition, the use of directional graphs allows each communication to be viewed in the "source/message/target" paradigm. This view of communication allows analysis of explicit and implicit influence content in the message. By examining the overall connectivity of the buying center, we get some indication of the efficiency of the group. Again, research with similar groups has shown that the greater the connectivity, the higher the problem-solving efficiency of the group. This measure would give some indication as to how much external communication it would take by a marketing organization to fully inform a potential organizational customer of the advantages of its product.

It is also an assumption of this research that the communication networks and influence patterns that evolve in the industrial purchasing process are not entirely unique but are subject to some general underlying forces that influence the structure of the buying center. These forces are the organizational setting within which the process takes place (the specific purchase situation) and individual differences of the participants. While structural aspects of the firm can be measured and a typology of product characteristics can be developed, understanding the individual differences of every buying-center participant and understanding how these differences affect the buying process seems to be an almost impossible task. Therefore, individual factors other than those of the purchasing manager will be ignored and treated as noise in the model formulation. The reason individual differences of the purchasing manager will be included is that this is a well-researched area and can provide additional tie-ins to previous, more traditional research.

Structural variables of the firm that are hypothesized to affect buying behavior are centralization, size, complexity, and formalization. Purchase-situation attributes that are hypothesized to affect buying-center composition are general product class, novelty of the purchase situation, complexity, and importance of the purchase. These variables are discussed at greater length in the section concerning independent variables in the chapter on methodology (Chapter 4).

Figure 3.1 presents a diagram of a hypothetical organization and a buying-decision communication network for a specific purchase. The communication links between those both within the firm and those external to it are depicted. In addition, the four criterion variables are depicted in relationship to the organization and the buying network. The four variables are (1) the vertical-hierarchy involvement in the buying network, (2) the lateral involvement of divisions and departments in the buying network, (3) the extension of the buying network or the number of individuals involved, and (4) the connectedness of those involved in the buying network (that is, the degree of connectivity of the entire network).

The vertical-structural dimension of organizational-buying behavior primarily concerns hierarchical distribution of authority for purchasing decisions. Identifying vertical levels of influence is clearly as important as any other dimension in the model. The vertical-influence dimension can be characterized by how extensively various management levels become involved in the purchasing process. The lateral-influence dimension is best understood as the number of separate departments, divisions, and/or functions that are involved in the purchase decision/communication network. When considered together, it should be clear why industrial buying behavior is perceived as a fuzzy set and why it has resisted attempts at analysis from a single-unit-of-analysis paradigm.

Lateral influence has often been referred to as "informal," while vertical influence has been considered "formal authority." However, in many organizations the lateral flow of influence has become formalized and is an important aspect of organizational-design considerations (Galbraith 1977). The relevance of lateral relations in purchasing as noted by Strauss (1962) was previously discussed. It should be remembered that he observed the tactics of purchasing agents who were subjected to strong influence from other functional areas. However, while Strauss emphasized the purchasing agents' attempts to strengthen their own positions, this analysis will identify the conditions under which such external influence is likely to exist. In addition, this analysis will determine when different levels of vertical authority are most likely to be involved in the purchase process.

Identification of these sources of influence is fundamental to the study of industrial buying behavior. Once locus of influence can be understood, further research may be directed at understanding the

FIGURE 3.1

A Communication Picture of a Buying Center

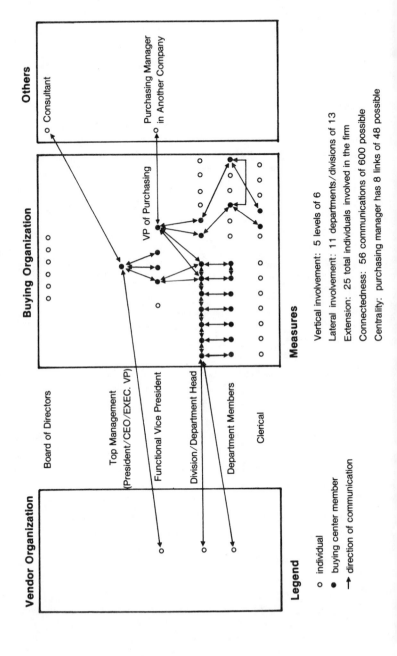

decision processes, examining bargaining modes among departments, information processing, and tactics of the various participants. An understanding of organization structure, however, is a necessary complement to analysis of the organizational process. The first two dimensions of buying behavior in industrial organizations (vertical and lateral) are structural dimensions. The second two dimensions (extension and connectedness) are more concerned with the group dynamics of the purchasing process.

Schroder, Driver and Streufert (1966) felt that information-processing systems could be described in terms of the number of parts at work (that is, people, departments) in a system and the amount of interconnection among parts. The term extension will be used in this book to describe what Schroder, Driver, and Streufert originally labeled differentiation or number of parts at work in the system. The greater the number of people involved in the industrial buying decision, the greater the extension of the buying center. Also, the greater the extension of the system, the more diffuse the locus of power or influence on the decision. The amount of interconnection among parts, originally termed integrative complexity by Schroder, Driver, and Streufert, will be referred to as connectedness. Connectedness is the degree to which the members of a group are linked with each other by communication flows. The actual degree of connectedness among the members of a group can be compared with the total possible degree of connectedness that could possibly exist. Because communication can be viewed as directional (source/message/target), directional graphs (digraphs) have been used to construct the communication networks; the highest possible degree of connectedness would exist when each individual was communicating to and receiving communication from every other member of the group. The degree of integration of a group has been associated with the quality of decisions. It is believed that the greater the connectedness of group members, the greater the amount of prior-information usage (Schroder, Driver, and Streufert 1966).

The relationship between the degree of internal connectedness and problem input is not simple, however. The basic Schroder, Driver, and Streufert model predicts that each system alters its internal, integrative complexity in a curvilinear manner as input complexity increases; therefore, systems have moderately complex optimal-input loads, which maximize their capacity for output quality. Stiles (1973), however, in his investigation of purchasing managers' information-processing behavior, found only a straight linear relationship between the number of participants in the decision process and the perceived quality of the outcome by the buyer.

Figure 3.2 depicts the buying-decision communication network separated from the organization's formal structure. It can be seen

FIGURE 3.2

Directed Graph of Communication in a Specific-Purchase Situation
(the Buying Center)

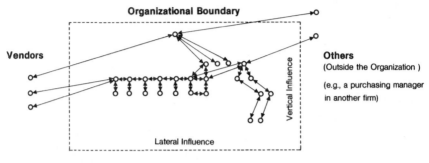

o   represents individuals
→ indicates the direction of communication

that five levels of vertical hierarchy are involved (vertical involvement), nine different divisions or departments are involved (lateral
involvement), a total of 25 different people within the firm are involved (task differentiation), and the degree of connectedness is
slightly less than 10 percent (integrative complexity); that is, there
are 56 communication links out of a possible 600.

A point should be made here about group connectedness (integrative complexity). As might be expected, larger-sized groups, all
other things being equal, have a lower degree of connectedness. This
is because it is more difficult for everyone in a larger group to communicate with everyone else. Therefore, the number of individuals
involved in a buying center must be taken into consideration when attempting to explain the connectedness of the purchasing-process participants.

In the next section, hypotheses will be developed concerning the
effect of situational and organizational-structural variables on the five
criterion variables discussed in this section: vertical involvement,
lateral involvement, extension, connectedness, and purchasing management's centrality.

HYPOTHESES AND DISCUSSION OF RATIONALE

Factors Affecting the Extent of Lateral Involvement in Buying Decisions

A common feature of complex organizations is horizontal differentiation of structure. This differentiation, when based on func-

tional specialties, is likely to lead to considerable lateral influence on buying decisions. The importance of other departments such as engineering, production, and finance in the purchasing process was illustrated by Strauss (1962). The involvement of these departments in the buying process could only occur if the organization consisted of such functional areas. The question arises, however, as to what organizational-structural dimensions and purchase-situation aspects lead to greater lateral involvement in the buying-decision process.

Organizational-Structural Variables and Their Hypothesized Effect on Lateral Involvement

Organizational Size. The relationship between the size of the organization and its degree of departmentalization is well established (Blau 1970). Larger organizations have greater flexibility in choosing the basis for grouping activities and frequently elect to form departments of functional specialists. Even within a single-product division, there is likely to be more functional differentiation as the division increases in size. In addition, there is the finding of correlation between the size of an organization and the number of boundary-spanning roles that exist within it (Aldrich and Herker 1977).

As size increases, so does the number of boundary-spanning roles. Because the purchasing process requires the interrelation of two parties (the buying organization and the seller), the purchasing function calls for boundary-spanning individuals. The existence and status of the purchasing department is, therefore, related to the size of the organization. The professionalism of purchasing personnel is likely to increase with greater specialization of the purchasing function. Differences between the purchasing department and other functional departments are also likely to increase to the point where what is best for the purchasing department is not necessarily optimal for the firm as a whole. Because purchasing and other specializations are interdependent, however, greater lateral influence is required in the purchasing process to ensure a better decision outcome. Considerable interaction and the need for coordination with other functions is a continuing reality for the purchasing department.

In summary, larger organizations are more departmentalized and contain more boundary-spanning roles than smaller organizations. This implies that the lateral influences on buying decisions are likely to be more extensive within larger organizations.

Hypothesis 1: The larger the size of an organization as measured by the number of employees or dollar sales, the greater the extent of lateral involvement in buying decisions.

Organizational Complexity. Complexity of organizations has been defined as the number of occupational specialties in the organization and their professionalism (Hage and Aiken 1970). As was seen in the last section, however, the relationship between the size of an organization and its structural complexity is well substantiated (Blau 1970). Larger organizations tend to be more structurally complex. Size is not a perfect substitute for organizational complexity, however. Therefore, this study will also consider the relationships between organizational complexity and other variables. In a highly complex organization, each individual has some latitude in designing his job to fit the task's needs. Close supervision is difficult to maintain because of the diverse nature in which individuals may define their tasks. The result, as Zaltman, Duncan, and Holbek (1973) point out, is that the individual has more of an opportunity to discover areas for innovation (and probably involvement). Complexity, therefore, will probably increase the informal influence in the purchasing process.

Hypothesis 2: The greater the complexity of an organization, the greater the extent of lateral involvement in buying decisions.

Organizational Formalization. Formalization has been defined as the emphasis placed on following specific rules and procedures in performing one's job within the organization (Zaltman, Duncan, and Holbek 1973). Strict emphasis on rigid rules and procedures may prohibit organizational decision makers from seeking new sources of information and also limit the extent of informal influence in purchasing decisions. On the other hand, formalization may require the interaction of various departments to ensure a completely coordinated purchase decision. Formalization, then, can be seen to affect how communication will take place but not necessarily whether it will affect the extent of lateral influence in the purchasing process. The more formalized an organization, the less the informal communication within it. Informal communication tends to be lateral and more often spoken than written.

Hypothesis 3: Formalization does not have an effect on lateral involvement in buying decisions. However, the greater the formalization of an organization, the more communication will tend to be written.

Organizational Centralization. Centralization can be viewed as having to do with the locus of authority and decision making in an organization. The greater the hierarchy of authority, that is, the higher up in the organization decision making takes place and the less participation there is in decision making within the organization, the greater the centralization of that organization. Greater lateral participation exists in decentralized organizations because of the need to gather input from each part of the organization. A common situation in purchasing for a highly decentralized company is to have an arrangement combining decentralization with some degree of centralization. In this type of operation "a staff manager for purchasing reports to the chief executive and is available at the request of operating divisions to help them with their problems" (Webster and Wind 1972, pp. 64-65).

Centralization should not be confused with geographical concentration. Centralization refers to decision-making locus of control, while geographical concentration refers to how physically close together are a business's operating locations. In a geographically dispersed company, purchasing decentralization would mean that different locations of the company would do their own purchasing. This would increase the lateral influence on purchasing decisions to individuals at each particular location.

Hypothesis 4: The greater the decentralization of the purchasing function, the greater the extent of lateral involvement in buying decisions.

Purchase-Situation Attributes and Their Hypothesized Effect on Lateral Involvement

The Importance of a Purchase. The importance of a purchase refers to the scope of that purchase relative to other purchases. The price of a purchase and the necessity of that product to the company's end product or output are dimensions of the importance of the purchase. In addition, the impact of the purchase on the different functions and individuals within the firm is also part of the purchase's importance. Patchen (1975) found that one of the most common reasons a person in an organization was influential in a purchase decision was because that person was in some way affected by the purchase; that is, the person had a stake in the outcome. The implication is that the greater the importance of a purchase, the greater the influence on buying decisions from a lateral extent. The more important purchases are in terms of total value, the greater the influence from production, quality control, and even marketing, because the consequences of the purchase are likely to pervade through to the price of the buying company's own product(s).

Hypothesis 5: The greater the perceived importance of a purchase, the greater the extent of lateral involvement in buying decisions.

The Complexity of a Purchase. The complexity of a purchase may be defined as the difficulty of understanding the features, operation, or other characteristics of the product or service. Increased purchase complexity may imply that the relevant knowledge is dispersed throughout the organization and not confined to the purchasing function. Thus, it could be expected that lateral influences will be greater for more complex purchases. Zaltman and Bonoma (1977) felt that "as products become more technologically innovative, the purchasing agent's central position declines" (p. 55). In another study of communication in the analysis of lateral influences in the purchase of a complex computer system, Pettigrew (1975) found that complexity increased lateral involvement.

Hypothesis 6: The greater the complexity of a purchase, the greater the extent of lateral involvement in buying decisions.

The Novelty of a Purchase. The more novel a purchase situation is for an organization, the less likely that a set purchase procedure exists for that product or service. In solving new problems more information tends to be examined than in solving routine or previously solved problems (Robinson, Faris, and Wind 1967). Mogee and Bean (1978) have made the following observation:

> In new purchases, technical personnel are most influential. They know what they want and generally how to bring it about, but they need information on the details in order to put their plans into form. They seek advice from colleagues in associated companies, non-commercial sources, and potential suppliers. In the early stages purchasing personnel play a largely information-providing role. [P. 135]

Hypothesis 7: The more novel a purchase situation is, the greater the extent of lateral involvement in buying decisions.

Factors Affecting the Vertical Distribution
of Involvement in Buying Decisions

The identification of lateral involvement in decision making is only the first of four dimensions necessary for full comprehension of the buying-center structure that evolves for a particular purchase within an organization. The vertical dimension is also important and varies with the same factors that influence lateral involvement.

Organizational-Structural Variables and Their
Hypothesized Effect on Vertical Involvement

Organizational Size. A number of studies show convincingly that
large organizations tend to be more decentralized, that is, decisions
are pushed downward in the organization (Child 1972; Mansfield 1973;
Robey, Bakr, and Miller 1977). This decentralization is accompanied
by increased standardization and formalization (Blau 1970; Child 1972;
Mansfield 1973). It very well may be that larger organizations adopt
bureaucratic strategies for controlling the outcomes of decentralized
decisions. Upper-level management still exerts influence, but only
indirectly, and would therefore not be involved in the communication
network. As lower-level roles become more structured via rules and
procedures, and if manuals exist to guide the decisions of purchasing
managers, then greater decentralization can occur without upper-level
management's loss of control over decision outcomes. Because larger
organizations are involved in many more decisions than smaller organizations, upper-level management has to rely on lower-level management to accomplish many tasks. In small organizations, top management is likely to make actual purchasing decisions. Because the
buying center is operationalized as the interaction between individuals
within the organization, size as measured by the number of individuals
employed by the organization will be a better measure for explanatory
purposes.

Hypothesis 8: (1) The larger the size of an organization, the
less the extent of vertical involvement in buying decisions and (2) size
as measured by number of employees will have a greater effect than
size as measured by sales revenue (dollars).

Organizational Complexity. The greater the number of occupational
specialties in an organization, and the more professionalism exhibited
by those specialties, the more complex an organization can be said to
be (Hage and Aiken 1970). The size of an organization is related to its
structural complexity. Gronhaug (1976) found a positive correlation
between size and the use of a separate purchasing department. As a
firm grows, the buying function becomes more specialized and increas-
ingly interdependent with other functions. There are other correlates
of organizational complexity, such as environmental diversity, but
the effect of organizational complexity on the extent of vertical involvement in buying decisions is similar to the effect on increase in size.
That is, in highly complex organizations, as in large organizations,
upper levels of management have less direct involvement in specific
functional tasks such as purchasing.

Hypothesis 9: The greater the complexity of an organization, the less the extent of vertical involvement in buying decisions.

Organizational Formalization. The more rules and procedures that exist in an organization, the less need there is for upper-level management to be directly involved in functional task areas. By having created the rules and procedures, upper-level management has attempted to exercise its prerogatives as to how a task should be accomplished.

Hypothesis 10: The greater the formalization of specific procedures in an organization, the less the extent of vertical involvement in buying decisions.

Organizational Centralization. Zaltman, Duncan, and Holbeck (1973) have defined organizational centralization by indicating that "the greater the hierarchy of authority (the higher in the organization decision making takes place) and less participation in decision making that exists in the organization, the greater the centralization" (p. 143). Thus, the participation of upper-level management would be greater by definition, in highly centralized organizations.

Hypothesis 11: The greater the centralization of an organization, the greater the extent of vertical involvement in buying decisions.

Purchase-Situation Attributes and Their
Hypothesized Effect on Vertical Involvement

The Importance of a Purchase. The more important purchases are in terms of total product value and organizational impact, the stronger the need for control over those purchases. Upper-level management will desire to have a direct input into such decisions. Vertical involvement is, therefore, likely to increase.

Hypothesis 12: The greater the perceived importance of a purchase, the greater the vertical involvement in buying decisions.

The Complexity of a Purchase. Complexity in a purchase situation is probably related to greater discretion at lower levels. The complexity of an item to be purchased requires expertise that may only be possessed by a technical specialist, whether in a purchasing department or elsewhere in the organization. As capital equipment and services become more complex, a more decentralized and nonbureaucratic structure is more appropriate overall (Perrow 1967).

Hypothesis 13: The greater the complexity of a purchase, the less the vertical involvement in buying decisions.

The Novelty of a Purchase. New purchases may also be classified as innovations. In organizational innovation, lower levels of the organization are most involved in initiation, while upper levels must be involved in implementation for success (Zaltman, Duncan, and Holbek 1973). For repetitive purchases where routine criteria and procedures may have become established, lower levels of the organization can function without direct supervision. Therefore, the more novel a purchase situation, the more likely higher-level management will feel the need to become involved because of the lack of structure and precedent.

Hypothesis 14: The more novel a purchase situation, the greater the vertical involvement in buying decisions.

Factors Affecting the Extension
of the Buying Center

While research has been conducted relating the amount of input complexity to system differentiation (Schroder, Driver, and Streufert 1966), little research has been conducted relating organizational-structural variables or purchase-situation attributes to the buying center's extension. Because of the definitions that have been developed of the organizational-structural variables and purchase-situation attributes, intuitive hypotheses would correlate organizational size and complexity positively with buying-center extension in purchasing decisions. Organizational centralization would correlate negatively with buying-center extension. The relationship between organizational formalization and extension is not clear, however. Because a stake in a purchase tends to bring participants into the purchase decision, it will be hypothesized that purchase importance is positively correlated with extension. Novelty of the purchase situation, or the lack of organizational expertise in decision making of that particular type, should increase the buying center's extension. The more complex the purchase decision, the greater the need to involve an increased number of organizational members and, therefore, the greater the buying center's extension.

Factors Affecting the Connectedness of the
Communication Network in Buying Decisions

Research has shown that the larger a network, the lower the connectedness (Berlo et al. 1972). Therefore, the size and complexity of an organization should correlate negatively with the connectedness of the various individuals involved in the purchase decision. Centralization should correlate positively with connectedness. The effect of formalization on connectedness is not clear. The importance of a purchase should increase the degree of buying-center connectedness because of the need for careful coordination. Novelty and complexity may correlate negatively because they would increase the extent of lateral involvement in the purchase decision and also the differentiation. On the other hand, with increased complexity or novelty in the purchase situation, the need for greater buying-center connectedness is clear. All other things being equal, it is hypothesized that novelty and complexity of the purchase situation will increase buying-center connectedness.

Factors Affecting the Centrality of the
Purchasing Department/Purchasing Manager
in the Communication Network

Because the communication network data are collected through the use of digraphs, which lend themselves readily to matrix algebra calculations, the centrality (status) of each individual can be calculated (Katz 1953). For this research only the centrality of the purchasing manager will be examined. The purchasing manager's status is expected to vary with the same organizational-structural variables and purchase-situation attributes previously discussed. The larger or more complex an organization, the more professional the purchasing function will tend to be and also the higher the status of the purchasing professional in the buying process. The more products or services are complex, new, or important, the lower will be the purchasing department's status in decisions. The effects of formalization and centralization are not clear.

CONCLUSION

This chapter began by examining the need to move away from the traditional research assumptions and approaches of industrial buying behavior for several reasons. The single unit of analysis has proved to be reductionistic and not particularly fruitful in empirical research attempts. A better conceptualization of industrial buying behavior would use communication relations or dyadic interaction as the basic unit of analysis and build a limited version of a general systems model of the buying center within the organization's formal boundary.

Five criterion variables in a dyadic-systems approach to industrial buying behavior were identified.

TABLE 3.1

Hypothesized Relationships between the Criterion Variables and the Predictor Variables

	Organizational Structural Variables				Purchase Situation Attributes		
	Size	Complexity	Formal-ization	Centralization	Importance	Novelty	Com-plexity
Vertical Involvement	-	-	-	+	+	+	-
Lateral Involvement	+	+	?	-	+	+	+
Extension	+	+	?	-	+	+	+
Connectedness	-	-	?	+	+	+	+
Centrality (status) of Purchasing	+	+	?	?	-	-	-

Legend: + = positive correlation, - = negative correlation, ? = effect uncertain.

1. Lateral involvement or the extent that various departments, divisions, or functional specialists become involved in the purchasing communication network;

2. Vertical involvement or the extent that various levels of the organizational hierarchy get involved in the purchasing-communication network;

3. Buying-center extension or the total number of individuals involved in the communication network;

4. Connectedness of the communication network or the extent to which individuals involved in the purchasing process are in communication with all others also involved; and

5. The centrality of the purchasing manager in the communication network.

Several organizational-structural variables and purchase-situation attributes were explored for hypothesized relationships to the criterion variables. Table 3.1 depicts the predicted relationships.

In the next chapter, the methodology used in the study of communication networks and influence patterns will be examined. This methodology includes a special sampling method of collecting data and the use of sociometric techniques to analyze the communication networks.

4

METHODOLOGY:
INVESTIGATING PATTERNS IN
INDUSTRIAL BUYING BEHAVIOR

This chapter outlines the methodology used to examine industrial buying behavior from a dyadic perspective. Particular sections discuss the sample of firms examined and how the individuals within each firm were identified and interviewed; the procedures used to collect the data; the variables, both criterion and predictor, to be used in the analysis; and the method of data analysis.

Because no two purchases in any given company will probably ever be exactly alike, nor will any two companies follow exactly the same procedure in two similar purchase situations, the process of each and every purchase is different. At the same time, there should be some general patterns of behavior and buying-center composition that will be the same for specific purchase situations. Similarities should also be observed across different companies with like structure buying the same goods and services. Communication strategies of marketers can and should take advantage of these general buying patterns. For instance, if it can be established that in the purchase of capital equipment the engineering function of the buying firm is usually consulted for its input, which might consist of anything from setting specifications to naming a particular supplier, then it would be essential for the firm marketing the equipment to attempt to communicate the advantages of their product's specifications and firm's reliability and service to the engineering department's personnel in the potential buying firms.

Likewise, by determining the extent of vertical and lateral involvement in the buying-decision process, the marketing organization has a better idea of who participates in the buying process and at what level decisions are being made and influence exerted. The marketer and sales representatives have more information about how to influence the potential transaction and how much of a selling job there remains to be successful. The centrality of the purchasing manager in the communication network indicates when, perhaps, selling the purchasing manager is sufficient to ensure the transaction. The connectedness and extension of the buying center can indicate how much effort must be exerted in communicating to all the individuals in the prospective customer firm and perhaps how quickly the information disseminated will spread throughout the buying center.

The research conducted in this study will attempt to determine who participates in the buying process, what influence they exert, and what conditions bring them into the buying center when capital equipment/machinery and industrial services are purchased. The reason for the selection of these two specific product categories is based upon wanting to select purchases that could vary enough on the three purchase-situation variables (importance, novelty, and complexity) to ensure the inclusion of the variables in the model to be constructed. While there are several theoretical product-purchase typologies, most categorizations of industrial products simply use a breakdown of five or six types of purchases (for example, raw materials, capital equipment/machinery, industrial services, supplies, and component parts). This categorization has remained more managerially useful in that it is readily identified and most managers have no difficulty in assigning purchases to these categories.

The data collected for this study consisted primarily of interviews with managers in actual ongoing companies involved in the purchase of goods and services, and the examination, where possible, of relevant documents (for example, letters, memoranda, and purchase requisitions) generated by the buying communication process.

In the next section, the sample of firms and their identification is discussed.

SUBJECTS AND SAMPLE CONSTRUCTION

The data sample consisted of interviews examining the purchase of different goods and services in a number of different organizations. Each organization from which data was collected was a for-profit firm in the private sector of the economy. Each firm was asked to provide information on two specific purchase decisions—one involving a piece of capital equipment or machinery and the other involving the purchase of industrial service. Where permitted, the files on the particular purchase were examined to corroborate the interview data and to provide a measure of the amount of communication that took place in a formal written manner. In all, about 35 organizations were contacted to participate in the study. Approximately 10 percent of the firms declined to participate or provided no usable data, although

certain individuals in the company did discuss purchasing in general
with the researcher. For the final analysis, only the 31 firms with
the most complete data will be used.

How the Sample Was Chosen

The National Association of Purchasing Managers (NAPM) was
contacted and asked to provide a list of purchasing managers and their
companies in the greater metropolitan area of Pittsburgh. The
secretary of the NAPM was willing to comply with the request after
the purpose and procedure of the research was explained to him.
Once the list was obtained, firms were identified using a number of
criteria. The two most important criteria were: (1) Was the firm a
for-profit, industrial manufacturer or distributor? and (2) Did the
firm contain one member who was affiliated with the NAPM? The reason for selecting firms that were either industrial manufacturers or
distributors was to ensure some reasonable degree of similar functions
across firms (for example, purchasing, engineering, marketing)
while at the same time allowing for diversity in the type of organization and types of product produced. The second criterion was required by default since only those individuals affiliated with the NAPM
appeared on the list provided by that agency. This is some ways
biased the sample toward companies with at least one functional
specialist in the purchasing area and, therefore, probably eliminated
the very smallest firms in the Pittsburgh area. Ammer (1968) provides evidence that the purchasing specialist does not begin to emerge
as a full-time position until the firm reaches the size of about 20
personnel.

Letters were sent by the director of corporate relations at the
University of Pittsburgh's Graduate School of Business to the individual
selected from each company with whom the data-collection process
was to begin. The letters explained the purpose of the study, the individuals involved, and the procedures of the interviewing process,
and requested the cooperation of the individual and his company in the
advancement of knowledge of industrial buying behavior.

The letters were followed within a week to ten days by a telephone call from the interviewer to set up an appointment for an interview if the individual was willing to participate in the study.

Because the sample of companies was small, entirely Pittsburgh
based, and composed of only those organizations with exceptionally
cooperative individuals, sample biases may exist and care must be
taken in generalizing the results beyond the scope of the data base.
The companies included, however, do represent considerable diversity in type of organization and product or service provided to the

TABLE 4.1

Sample of Companies by Primary Product or Service Produced

Company 1	Chemical Producer	
Company 2	Industrial Safety Products Manufacturer	
Company 3	Steel Mill Furnace Manufacturer	
Company 4	Steel Manufacturer	
Company 5	Water Transportation and Construction Company	
Company 6	Heating Equipment Manufacturer	
Company 7	Industrial Products Distributor	
Company 8	Specialty Steel Manufacturer	
Company 9	Machine Tooling Company	
Company 10	Specialty Steel Manufacturer	
Company 11	Industrial Products Distributor	
Company 12	Metal and Wire Manufacturer	
Company 13	Aerospace and Automotive Products Manufacturer	
Company 14	Paper Products Manufacturer	
Company 15	Steel Mill Builder	
Company 16	Refractory	
Company 17	Pipe Fabricator	
Company 18	Petroleum Products Manufacturer	
Company 19	Power Plant Builder	
Company 20	Steel Manufacturer	
Company 21	Cement Manufacturer	
Company 22	Mining Equipment Manufacturer	
Company 23	Chemical and Scientific Instrument Distributor	
Company 24	Electric Parts Distributor	
Company 25	Steel Fabrication	
Company 26	Construction Company	
Company 27	Steel Manufacturer	
Company 28	Engineering and Construction Company	
Company 29	Home Products Manufacturer	
Company 30	Electrical Parts Manufacturer	
Company 31	Building Materials Manufacturer	

market. In addition, considerable variation was found within the organizational-structural variables of size, complexity, formalization, and centralization. Table 4.1 provides a list of the sample companies by primary product or service produced.

Identifying the Purchase Situations for Study

At each company that agreed to participate in the study, the individual to whom the letter of introduction had been sent was asked to identify a specific purchase of, first, capital equipment and, then, an industrial service made recently by the individual's company in which the individual had been involved. If the person with whom initial contact had been made had not been involved in the purchase of either capital equipment or an industrial service, he was asked to provide the name of another individual within the company who might have been involved in such a purchase. By using this technique, it was possible to identify persons involved in the purchase of both capital equipment and industrial services within each company.

It is important to point out several aspects of this means of purchase-situation selection. Because protocol analysis and interviews of company personnel involved in the purchase were to be used, it was important to select a purchase that had recently transpired for several reasons: the process involved in the purchase, including the various communications that took place, would be fresher in the minds of those individuals involved and, therefore, more easily recalled; and the individuals involved were much more likely to still be connected with the firm and in the same position as when the purchase took place. The first point was important to ensure as complete a recall from each individual as possible, and the second point was important to ensure as complete a sample response within each company as possible. In addition, because no dollar range was specified for either purchase situation, a greater variation of purchase value was obtained. The dollar value of a purchase was felt to be correlated with the importance or scope of that purchase. In addition, by asking for a recent purchase rather than a particular type of equipment or service purchase, it was possible to get a more generalizable sample of purchase situations. The purchase situations obtained through this technique varied considerably along all three purchase-situation attributes (importance, novelty, and complexity). Purchases of each of the three categories (new task, modified rebuy, and straight rebuy) developed by Robinson, Faris, and Wind (1967) can be identified. These purchases varied considerably in the amount of deliberation about what type of product and supplier to select.

It must still be pointed out, however, that because of the unsystematic purchase-situation selection, the specific situations included in this study cannot be said to be strictly representative of any specific universe of purchase situations. One important bias that must be mentioned is the fact that, with the exception of only one purchase of capital equipment and three service purchases, the initial contact person was a purchasing specialist, and, therefore, most situations include the presence or involvement of the purchasing function. There are few purchases of capital equipment that would not include some involvement of the purchasing department; however, the purchase of services is another issue. Several important purchases of services by companies, such as an annual audit by a public accounting firm or the services of an advertising agency, could very possibly

TABLE 4.2

Purchases Made by Sample Companies

Company	Capital Equipment/Machinery	Industrial Services
1	Heat Exchanger	Construction Contract Labor
2	Automatic Drilling Machine	Plant Janitorial Service
3	Standby Oil Heating System	Temporary Drafting Help
4	Coke Oven	Maintenance Repair Contract
5	Locomotive Crane	Contracted Cement Work
6	Large Industrial Press	Refuse Removal
7	Heater Plasma Cutting Equipment	Installation of Fire Prevention System
8	Hot Piercer Mill	General Contractor for Asphalt Work
9	Vertical Boring Mill	Fabricating Work
10	Steel Plate Leveler	Calibration of Lab Instruments
11	Storage Shelving	Refuse Removal
12	Wrapping Machine	Machinery Rigging for Shipping
13	Metal Working Machine Tool	Technical Consultant
14	Banding System	Vending Machine Service
15	Processing Pump	Pump Installation & Start Up
16	Fork-Lift Trucks	Plant Security Protection
17	Presses	Janitorial Contract Service
18	Gasoline Storage Tank	Printing of Advertising Materials
19	Nuclear Load Cell	External Building Maintenance
20	River Tow Barge	Employee Food Service
21	Fork-Lift Truck	Plant Security Protection
22	Executive Office Desk	Training for 1st Line Supervisors
23	Medical Instruments	Management Consultant
24	Recessed Lighting Fixtures	Architectural Services
25	Bar Stock Steel	Typewriter Maintenance
26	Steel Tonnage	Site Survey
27	Galvanized Steel Processor	Processing Slag & Metal Recovery Service
28	Cooling Vessel	Tar Sludge Removal
29	Mixing Machines	Drapery Cleaning
30	Resister	Refuse Removal
31	Pump	Engineering Services

be made without any involvement of the purchasing department. It should be remembered, however, that the purchase was specified to be an industrial service, and, therefore, most services identified were connected with production and/or maintenance. Table 4.2 presents a list of the type of capital equipment and industrial service examined in each firm. It seems likely that these purchases are reasonably representative of purchases in the specific categories examined in this study.

DATA-COLLECTION PROCEDURES

The data-collection methodology consisted of identifying one individual in each firm who was involved in some way in the communication network generated by the interaction of the buying-center members in the purchase of each product. This individual was usually from the purchasing or materials-management department. The interviews were semistructured and attempted to identify all those individuals with whom the individual being interviewed communicated and what the content of those communications was. Appendix 1 contains a copy of the interview schedule used. Each individual's role and tasks in the purchasing process were also recorded. Protocol analysis (having the individual attempt to describe what happened in the process) was used.

After identifying and structuring the entire part this individual played in the purchasing process, the other individuals identified as having had contact with this person were contacted and interviewed to fill in their part in the buying process. This is similar to what is referred to as "snowball" sampling. Interviews with one individual involved in the purchasing process led to interviews with other individuals involved in the process, which led to the identification and subsequent interview of still others. This expanding-interview process eventually exhausted itself when all the individuals within a firm who had a part in the purchasing process were identified and interviewed. Individuals outside the buying organization who had contact with individuals inside the organization have been diagramed in the communication network but not interviewed. The communication networks involved anywhere from three individuals (one individual involved in buying, one in product/service-need identification, and one in selling) to over 20 (numerous participants involved in the buying center and several selling-organization representatives). The length of the protocol-analysis procedure and completion of the interviewing process in each firm for the two purchases examined took about two to three days.

The intention of the interview process was, originally, to follow the flow of communications concerning each purchase and conduct interviews with each person within the buying firm who had any involvement in the process. This snowball interview technique was, because of certain individual and organizational constraints, only partially successful. It was not always possible to interview everyone who had been involved in the process. A certain reluctance existed on the part of some of the purchasing managers initially contacted to provide the names and telephone extensions or addresses of the other individuals involved in the purchasing process. While the purchasing manager was fully willing in almost every case to spend any amount of time answering questions, he usually had only a partial picture of the total-purchase process. When it was pointed out that certain questions had to be asked of others in the firm, the purchasing manager was usually willing to provide the names of only one or two others who had been involved in the process. It was also sometimes impossible to interview specific persons for various reasons such as their refusal to participate, being out of the country, or having died.

In most companies, permission was obtained to interview those persons who had significant involvement in a purchase decision, but not those peripherally involved. In most cases, it was found to be relatively easy to trace the persons involved in the buying process. By using the purchasing department's file on the specific purchase and examining the written documents, such as purchase requisitions, it proved possible to develop a clear picture of the purchase process and the communication network generated by it.

In every company, it proved possible to interview enough persons connected with each purchase decision to get a sufficiently detailed description of how the decision evolved. In addition, the protocols of various organizational members showed a high degree of consistency, hopefully indicating a certain degree of validity for the observations. It is important to note here that others using this same technique (Gronhaug 1977; Patchen 1969) have also reported a high degree of convergence in subjects' responses. In the studies discussed in Chapter 2 using influence ratings and other studies trying to identify general involvement in purchasing procedures (Harding 1966; Walsh 1961), difficulties in identifying the persons involved in the buying process and their influence have been discovered. Apparently, this inconsistency may be due to the examination of specific purchase situations versus a generalized approach to purchasing participation.

The interview procedure proved to be relatively successful even though not everyone could be interviewed. A total of 241 interviews were conducted in the 62 purchase situations within the 31 companies. Some situations had as low as only two individuals involved who could be interviewed. A minimum of two individuals were interviewed in each situation and the average was four individuals per purchase decision. Interviews were conducted both in person and by telephone. The interviewee was usually allowed to determine which type of interview he preferred. Some interviews out of the Pittsburgh area had to be conducted by telephone.

One interesting outcome of the protocol analysis was the tendency for different functional specialists to be more detailed in the specification of some of the steps involved in the purchase process than in others. Specifically, engineers tended to be more detailed in their task-step analysis than purchasing managers. The key to the appropriate level of task aggregation lies in the salient perceptions of the organizational members; that is, what the individuals perceived to be the level of task definition was accepted. Although this type of investigation is extremely time intensive, it is the best approach for the current level of development in this area.

INTERVIEWS

In using interviews as a tool of scientific research, the question of whether data can be obtained in an easier or better way must be asked. In this particular case, the answer is no. A questionnaire would save time, but the purpose of this research is to identify the participants in the purchasing process; the questionnaire would therefore have to be administered to everyone in the organization. The interview, on the other hand, can be used as an exploratory device to help identify individuals and the relationships existing between them as well as the tasks each one performs. The interview is considered a psychological and sociological measuring implement. More accurately, the product of interviews (the respondents' answers to the carefully developed protocol analysis) can be translated into measures of variables. Interviews are therefore subject to the same criteria of reliability, validity, and objectivity as any other measuring instruments.

The type of interview used to collect the necessary data for this research was semistructured, with certain parts allowing for unstandardized responses. The basic questions the interview strived to examine were, What happened in the buying process? How was each respondent involved? and Who did the respondent interact with? When these questions were answered by each person in the firm involved in the purchasing process, digraphs were constructed to visually depict the process.

MEASURES OF INTEREST

Criterion Variables

The major dependent variables can all be obtained from the communication network through either observational techniques or the use of matrix algebra. The following is a description of the variables to be obtained, the method for calculating them, and their meaning or use in understanding the functioning of the buying center.

Vertical Involvement

The degree of vertical involvement in a purchase situation can be measured by the number of hierarchical-authority levels exerting influence or communicating within the buying organization. An equally important consideration for the marketing organization is the highest level exerting influence within the buying organization. For the purposes of developing a comparable measure of vertical involvement, the hierarchical-authority levels have been divided into six standard levels. These levels are the following:

Ownership (represented by the board of directors in large companies),
Top management (chief executive officer, president, executive vice-
    president),
Policy-level management (functional vice-president),
Upper-level operating management,
Lower-level operating management (first-level supervisors),
Production worker/clerical-level employees.

Each of the 31 firms in this research contained these 6 levels of hierarchical authority. This variable is measured by simple observation of the communication network to determine the number of levels of authority participating in the decision and the highest level involved.

Lateral Involvement

The degree of lateral involvement in a purchase decision can be measured by the number of different departments and divisions exerting influence or involved in the communication network within the buying organization. This is an important consideration for the industrial marketer, because it gives an indication of the potential for diversity of opinion and the possibility for influencing the decision through a number of functional areas within the firm. If purchasing, engineering, production, and maintenance departments are involved in the purchase decision, the marketer can attempt to influence all or only some of these functions. Certainly the greater the number of functional areas involved, the greater the marketer's job in selling his product to the particular firm. No standard number of departments or divisions was developed for the 31 firms involved in the study. Each firm was sufficiently departmentalized to contain a purchasing function and most had more than one plant or operating location. The degree of lateral involvement is measured by simple observation of the communication network to determine the number of different departments and divisions/plants involved in the communication process for the specific purchase decision.

Extension

The degree of extension of the buying center is in some ways related to the extent of lateral and vertical involvement in the purchase-decision process but is a measure of involvement in its own right. Extension is a measure of the total number of individuals involved in the buying center; that is, while there may be only one level of vertical involvement and only two departments (purchasing and engineering) involved in a purchase decision, the degree of extension may vary from only one member of each department being involved up to any number of individuals from the two departments. The degree of extension is defined by how many individuals are involved in the buying center. This variable is measured by observation of the communication network to determine how many individuals were involved in the purchase decision. It has been hypothesized (Schroder, Driver, and Streufert 1966) that system differentiation (extension) is correlated with input complexity and output quality.

Connectedness

Connectedness is the degree to which the members of a group are linked or connected with each other by communication flows. For the purposes of this research, the actual degree of connectedness among the individuals of the buying center was compared with the total possible degree of connectedness that could potentially exist. The amount of connectedness of a group has usually been thought to be correlated with the speed of diffusion of information. Therefore, the greater the connectedness of a buying center, the greater the rapidity of marketing communications spreading through the buying center. For buying centers with a low connectivity, the marketing communication process needs to be directed at more members of the firm. Figure 4.1 provides an illustration of different degrees of buying-center connectedness.

This variable is also measured by observing the communication network of the buying organization and determining how many communication links exist as a ratio of the total possible.

FIGURE 4.1

An Illustration of Different Degrees of Buying-Center Connectedness

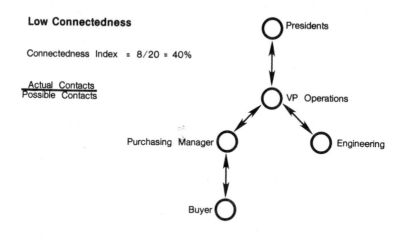

Low Connectedness

Connectedness Index = 8/20 = 40%

$\dfrac{\text{Actual Contacts}}{\text{Possible Contacts}}$

Presidents

VP Operations

Purchasing Manager

Engineering

Buyer

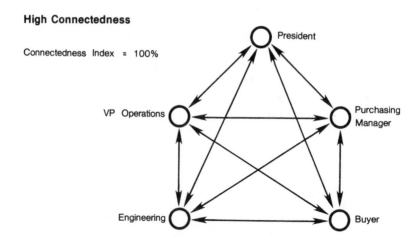

High Connectedness

Connectedness Index = 100%

President

VP Operations

Purchasing Manager

Engineering

Buyer

Centrality of Purchasing (Status)

The relative centrality of any decision-making participant can be developed out of the communication network using matrix algebra. By depicting the communication digraph as an $n \times n$ matrix, the ability to use matrix algebra is developed.

The simplest technique to describe the purchasing manager in the buying center is to use the sum of his rows and columns in the communication matrix. This, however, makes it difficult to compare individuals in buying centers of different sizes. Various refinements exist, such as weighting the sum for the individual's input/output in the matrix by the maximum number it is possible for him to send or receive. The simple row-column index, however, does not take into account indirect as well as direct links between the members of the buying center. There may be an important difference in the purchasing manager's status, depending upon the centrality or status of those he communicates with or receives communication from.

Katz (1953) developed a status index that takes account of such indirect links. In a matrix with binary entries, the powers of the matrix give the number of indirect connections to each member of the group. The entries in the squared matrix indicate the number of two-link connections between each pair of group members. Cubing the original matrix would give a matrix all of whose entries would indicate the number of three-link connections, and so on. The status index (T) for each individual is computed as the total of all direct and indirect links to the individual. These may be obtained from the column sums of the original matrix plus those of all the powers of the matrix.

$$T = A + A^2 + A^3 + \ldots + A^k + \ldots \tag{1}$$

It can be demonstrated, however, that equation 1 is equivalent to

$$T = (I - A)^{-1} - I \tag{2}$$

where A is the original sociometric matrix with zeroes in the diagonal and I is the identity matrix.

Katz further suggests that indirect links should be weighted inversely to the number of links involved. To do this a constant (C) is employed with $0 < c < 1$. The following formula then gives the matrix of summed and weighted values:

$$T = cA + c^2A^2 + \ldots + c^kA^k + \ldots \tag{3}$$

There is an equivalent formula for the computation of status that finds the solution through a set of linear equations rather than by finding the inverse of the matrix explicitly.

$$(1/cI - A')t = s \tag{4}$$

where A´ is the transpose of A, and s is a column vector whose entries are the column sums of A. The formula yields a set of linear equations that may be solved for t, the sums of the columns of T.

The inverse matrix of I - cA can be taken to summarize the eventual effect of each member of the others. One unit of activity or communication will give rise to a fraction of a unit's activity by other members. The row sums indicate the long-run influence of each member. The column sums may be taken to signify the amount of constraint or pressure put on each member in the long run. It is also possible to estimate the effect of various distributions of input from the external environment using this matrix technique. If each member of the buying center were to receive one unit of external input, say an advertising message, that he relays to members of the buying center, the eventual effect of each member can be computed by postmultiplying $(I - cA)^{-1}$ by a column vector of ones. The effect of differences in the amount of external input can be similarly computed by postmultiplying with the appropriate column vector containing a different distribution of inputs.

The importance of the centrality of the purchasing manager to industrial marketers should be clear. The purchasing manager is often the most easily reached member of the buying center for the sales representative. When the purchasing manager's centrality is high, it may be sufficient to sell only him on one's product; but when the purchasing manager's centrality is low, it would be beneficial to attempt to contact other members of the buying center.

For the purposes of this research, the measure of purchasing managers' centrality will be the row and column sum from the $(I - cA)^{-1}$ matrix divided by 2. This measure combines the amount of communication an individual sends and receives, and weights are according to the size of the group and how much information he could have sent and received.

Predictor Variables

The predictor, or independent, variables will consist of measurements of two different situational aspects of the company-purchase interaction. The first class of variables will be those that measure various structural aspects of each organization. The second set of measurements will examine aspects of the purchase-situation attributes.

Structural Dimensions of Organizations

Research on organizational-structural dimensions has concentrated on five dimensions of structure.

1. Centralization refers to the degree to which authority, responsibility, and power are concentrated within an organization.
2. Formalization refers to the extent to which activity in an organization is formally outlined by rules and procedures.

3. Complexity refers to the degree to which the organization is compartmentalized by departments and divisions and functions are specialized.

4. Size refers to how large the organization is in comparison to other organizations.

5. Participation in decision making refers to the extent to which various organizational members are involved in decision making.

Since the dependent variables of this research already measure several aspects of participation in organizational decision making, an independent variable to measure organizational structure will not be included. Thus, the organizational-structural variables of interest in this research are centralization, formalization, complexity, and size.

Organizational Centralization. Organizational centralization can be conceptualized as the locus of authority and decision making in an organization (Zaltman, Duncan, and Holbek 1973). The higher in the organization decision making takes place and the less participation there is, the greater the centralization of that organization. The operationalization of organizational centralization was accomplished through two questions pertinent to the purchasing function. The reason these questions dealt only with purchase-decision making is that various decision areas within a firm can be at different levels of centralization and the dependent variables deal only with the purchasing function and the buying center.

The two questions that measured organizational centralization of purchasing were, What level in the company is the purchasing department? and How is the purchasing function organized within the company?

Organizational Formalization. The emphasis placed on following rules and procedures in the performance of a task is the substance of organizational formalization. The existence of rules and procedures is also an indication of formalization. In addition, for this research the percentage of communication that is generated in written form is a measure of formalization. The greater the amount of written communication concerning the purchase of goods and services, the greater the formalization of the process.

The following measures were used to operationalize the concept of organizational formalization:

1. The existence of a purchasing-policies manual in the company,

2. If there were dollar limits various ranks in purchasing needed authorization to commit and what the lowest limit was,

3. The percentage of written versus spoken communication generated by the buying center in the purchasing-decision process, and

4. The average of perceptions of the buying-center members concerning the degree of formalization of their companies' purchasing policies/procedures in comparison with other companies.

Organizational Complexity. The complexity of an organization is a function of the degree to which the organization is compartmentalized and functions are specialized.

The following measures were used to operationalize the concept of organizational complexity: the number of organizational divisions and the number of separate plants and operating locations.

These two measures were designed to examine the degree of organizational compartmentalization.

Organizational Size. The size of an organization has been successfully operationalized by using the net sales and the number of employees (Peters and Venkatesan 1973). Both of these variables were found to be significant when testing the hypothesis that the size of the firm would be positively related to adoption of a computer. While their research dealt with the purchase of an innovation, it is expected that size can be operationalized in the same manner for the research of this study. Therefore, size will be measured as the net sales (dollars) of the firm and the number of employees of the firm.

Purchase-Situation Attributes

There has been little research into purchase-specific situational attributes such as the product class, or the importance, novelty, and complexity of the product to the buying firms. This research examined purchases made from the two product classes of capital equipment and industrial services. Purchases from these classes were allowed to vary on the dimensions of importance, novelty, and complexity.

Product Classification. Buying assignments within a purchasing department are often specific (item by item) with a definite responsibility for each item or commodity classification that is regularly purchased. So far as is practical, items that are related by nature or by source (rather than by end product or using department) are grouped for buying purposes. In effect, there can be no standard purchasing classification of commodities that will be applicable to all companies. Requirements vary widely among different industries, but a classification by product class should be applicable to the widest group of companies. The six product classes often used to group the many possible purchases organizations make are raw materials, pre-fabricated materials, supplies, component parts, capital equipment, and services. The two product classes of capital equipment and industrial services were selected to explore for differences in buying-center composition and individual-member status as a function of the product class being purchased.

Attributes of the Purchase Situation. There has been little attempt to generate a systematic set of purchase-situation attributes and to relate them to buying behavior in organizations. When a typology is based on a primary attribute, a purchase can be confidently classified without reference to a specified organization. Regardless of its size, wealth, complexity, decentralization, and so forth, each organization would place the purchase in the same cell of the typology. When a typology is based on a secondary attribute, however, the classification of the purchase depends on the organization involved in the buying process (Downs and Mohr 1972). Influences on buying decisions may vary with the secondary attributes of contemplated purchases rather than with their objective or primary characteristics. The same purchase is likely to be perceived differently by two buyers because of the secondary attributes, which can be different for each firm. Secondary attributes are described by words such as complexity, novelty, and importance, whereas primary attributes are described in terms of cost, size, shape, and color.

Importance of a Purchase. The importance of a purchase refers to the scope of that purchase relative to other purchases made by the firm. Importance was operationalized by measuring and averaging the perceptions of the buying-center members as to how important the particular purchase was if compared with the other purchases their company made.

Complexity of a Purchase. The complexity of a purchase may be defined as the difficulty of understanding the features, operation, or other characteristics of the product and purchase situation. Complexity is probably inversely related to the product knowledge possessed by the buying organization.

Complexity was operationalized by averaging the responses of the buying-center members to a question regarding the perceived complexity or difficulty in evaluating the alternatives available for the particular purchase.

In addition, the number of vendors involved and offers obtained may correlate with the perceived difficulty of purchase evaluation. This variable was also measured and will be involved in the study. The time from first recognition of need to installation or performance evaluation was also measured and may correlate with complexity.

<u>Novelty of a Purchase</u>. The third purchase attribute is the novelty of the purchase situation to the buying organization. Completely new purchases may also be classified as innovations, according to some definitions. Evidence suggests that different buying influences exist for repetitive purchases where routine criteria and procedures have become established (Robinson, Faris, and Wind 1967). Novelty was operationalized by measuring the first and most recent purchase of the product and the frequency of the particular buying situation. A categorization of purchase situations as new task, modified rebuy, and straight rebuy (Robinson, Faris, and Wind 1967) was also accomplished and used as an independent variable.

DATA ANALYSIS

The most important relationships examined in this research involved buying-center composition, organizational-structural variables, and purchase-situation attributes. While it is difficult to pre-specify the form of the model, it was felt that a linear, additive relationship could exist between the dependent and independent variables and that a multiple-regression analysis technique was appropriate for the analysis of the data.

Each of the dependent variables was examined for the effect of the independent variables. The form of the equations was as follows:

Dependent Variable (Vertical Involvement, Lateral Involvement, Differentiation, Integration, Centrality of the Purchasing Manager) = b_1 Organizational Centrality + b_2 Organizational Formalization + b_3 Organizational Complexity + b_4 Organizational Size + b_5 Purchase Importance + b_6 Purchase Novelty + b_7 Purchase Complexity.

In analyzing the centrality of the purchasing manager involved in the purchase, a number of personal measures were taken of the particular purchasing manager.

The purchasing manager's position in the company,
Length of time worked for the company,
Length of time worked in purchasing area for the company,
Years of purchasing experience,
Level of education,
Whether or not the individual is a certified purchasing manager,
Number of people in the purchasing department,
Level of the purchasing department in the company.

These measures were incorporated into the analysis to examine the centrality of the particular purchasing manager.

CONCLUSION

This chapter has detailed the methodology of this study including the sample and its selection, the procedure of data collection, the major variables of interest, and the method of data analysis.

The purchase of products of 31 firms from two different product classes were investigated. In all, over 240 interviews were conducted. The method of interviewing can be referred to as snowballing because the sampel begins with one individual within the organization and grows as more and more people involved in the buying process are identified.

The major variables of interest are those that measure buying-center composition as it is affected by organizational-structural variables and purchase-situation attributes.

Regression analysis was used to examine the relationship between variables and the amount of variance in the buying-center composition explained by the independent measures.

In the next chapter the results of this research are discussed from both a technical, research-oriented perspective and also from a more qualitative viewpoint.

5

ANALYSIS OF THE
DYADIC-SYSTEMS APPROACH TO
INDUSTRIAL BUYING BEHAVIOR:
RESULTS AND DISCUSSION

This chapter presents the results of the data analysis of this study from both a quantitative and qualitative perspective. An in-depth discussion of the meaning of the results runs parallel to the presentation of those results. The quantitative and qualitative findings of this study are felt to be equally important. The quantitative analysis of the data addresses some of the critical questions of this study, formulated as hypotheses in Chapter 3. The quantitative results allow prediction and possible control of the dimensions of the buying-center system within customer organizations. Important results of this study are also found in the qualitative analysis of the data. This type of analysis and its findings are reported in the sections dealing with the process of industrial buying behavior and the in-depth analysis of the various stages found within the framework of industrial buying. The more qualitative findings allow greater understanding of the buying process within organizations and extend the knowledge of marketing in the industrial buying-behavior area.

The examination of the dimensions of the buying-center system within an organization permit the marketer to develop strategic communication tools to reach a greater number of those individuals involved in the buying-decision process. The understanding of the buying process enables the marketer to know who exerts what type of influence at particular phases in the buying process.

This chapter is organized as follows. The first section examines descriptive information of the companies, purchase situations, and markets for capital equipment and industrial services involved in this study. The second section analyzes the buying-center system's dimensions using stepwise linear regression for both capital-equipment and industrial-service purchases. The third section aggregates the communication networks of each company into two composite matrixes, one for capital-equipment purchases and one for industrial-service purchases. These matrixes allow the examination of the participation of various functional areas in the buying center for various product categories and also the intercommunication, dyad formation, that takes place in the buying process for the different product categories. The fourth section presents a qualitative analysis of the industrial buying process for each product category and compares and contrasts this with the traditional literature concerning the steps, stages, and phases of industrial buying behavior. This section concludes with a chart showing the involvement of the various functional areas in the different tasks required in the industrial buying process.

The total product of this chapter is an examination of the communication networks and influence patterns of industrial buying behavior. The model and hypotheses of Chapter 3 are examined and tested with the hope of providing a better understanding of industrial buying behavior via a new conceptualization. The dyadic-systems model should provide management with important information and insights into the buying-center system and its functioning. This information and understanding will enable management to develop better industrial-marketing communication programs and strategic approaches to organizational customers.

BASIC SAMPLE STATISTICS AND DESCRIPTIVE INFORMATION

Before moving into the quantitative and qualitative analyses, it seems necessary to examine some of the basic statistics of the sample firms, the purchase situations, and some descriptive information concerning the overall nature of the data. By doing this, the generalizability of the case studies accomplished in this research can be examined. In addition, description of the data will be useful for developing a better feeling for the nature and scope of industrial buying-behavior processes.

Structural Variables of the Firms

Size of the Companies Involved

The companies from which data were collected were in the medium-to-large range of companies for sales and number of employees. Several of the companies were listed within the Fortune 500 largest companies in the United States. With the exception of the privately owned companies, all companies were listed in either the Dun and

Bradstreet Million Dollar Directory or Middle Market Directory.
One privately owned company would not release either its net sales
figure or the number of employees it had, but it is estimated that this
company would have been within the ranges established by the other
companies; that is, the one company for which sales and employee
statistics are not available is not believed to be either smaller or
larger than the smallest and largest companies in the sample.

Net sales of the companies in this study ranged from $5 million
to $8.6 billion. The median figure for companies' sales was $300
million.

Employees of the companies numbered from 59 for the smallest
to over 160,000 in the largest. Four companies employed less than
1,000 workers. The mean number of employees for companies in the
sample was 27,000. The median figure was 4,000.

Complexity of the Companies Involved

The complexity of the companies involved was measured by the
number of divisions and subsidiaries each company was divided into
as well as the total number of separate operating locations and plants.
Six companies had only one operating location and were not division-
alized nor had any subsidiaries. The number of divisions and subsidiaries for the companies in the sample ranged from just 1 to 39
for the most complex company. Separate operating locations and
plants ranged in number from 1 to over 200. The median number of
divisions and subsidiaries for the companies surveyed was five. The
median number of separate operating locations and plants was 12.

The Primary Business of the Companies

Two companies served end-consumer markets primarily. Four
companies were distributors of industrial products. The rest of the
sample (25 firms) were producers of industrially bought goods and
services. All of the companies contained departments with functional
specialists in the purchasing area.

Organizational Formalization

Of the 31 companies in the sample, 9 had no company manual
of purchasing procedures and policies. The other 22 companies had
purchasing manuals that ranged from simple pamphlets up to several-
volume editions including flow chart diagrams explicitly structuring
the flow of the buying process for specific goods and services.

Nine of the companies had no dollar restrictions placed upon
purchasing personnel concerning the maximum amount of funds they
were authorized to commit before securing the approval of the next

TABLE 5.1

Dollar Limits for Various Ranks in Functional Areas

Purchasing Rank/Authorization Limit			Engineering Rank/Authorization Limit		
Buyer	up to	$5,000	Requisition/Shop Order Holder	up to	$1,000
Senior Buyer	"	$25,000	Engineer	"	$5,000
Senior Procurement Specialist		$50,000	Engineering Staff Manager	"	$25,000
			Project Manager	"	$50,000
Procurement Manager		$100,000	Department Head (Services)	"	$100,000
Purchasing Manager		$250,000	Projects Department Manager (Department Head)	"	Any Amount
Manager of Purchasing and Traffic (Department Manager)		Any Amount			

level of management. In the 22 companies that had dollar-limit restrictions, these limits were as high as $50,000. Three companies had limits under $1,000. One of these companies required all purchases made by the lowest level of purchasing specialist to be approved by a higher level of purchasing management. The median dollar limit for all companies was $5,000. Sometimes dollar limits were in effect only when the purchase under consideration had not been made by the particular company before; that is, when a product or service being considered for purchase was novel to the company, certain preestablished dollar limits were imposed upon the various ranks in purchasing management. Limits were also imposed on other functional-area specialists in some companies. For instance, engineering department managers were often required to seek higher-level approval of designs and specifications for a purchase under consideration if that purchase exceeded the dollar limit they were authorized to approve. Table 5.1 gives an example of this dollar-limit structuring in company 19 (power plant builder).

The perceived formality of the companies' purchasing policies and procedures varied from "not at all formalized" to "extremely formalized." This judgment was made in comparison to other companies. The mean response on an interval scale from 1 to 10 was 7. Perceived formalization of purchasing policies/procedures correlated positively with company size, as measured by both sales and employees ($r = .39$, $p < .02$; $r = .46$, $p < .01$, respectively) and the size of the purchasing department ($r = .24$, $p < .10$). Higher levels of management were less likely to view the company's purchasing policies/procedures as being formalized ($r = -.42$, $p < .01$). The longer a purchasing manager had worked for a company, the less formalized he perceived the purchasing procedures and policies to be $(r = -.27, p < .07)$.

The absolute amount of written communication generated by a purchase decision varied positively with the perceived importance of the purchase and the time it took to accomplish the entire buying-decision process, from first-recognized need to purchase and evaluation. The ratio of written communication versus spoken communication correlated positively with how often that particular type of purchase was made $(r = .30, p < .05)$ and how many vendors were involved in the purchase decision $(r = .29, p < .06)$. The percentage of communication that was written correlated negatively with the importance $(r = -.26, p < .08)$ and complexity $(r = -.28, p < .07)$ of a purchase situation; that is, the more important and/or complex a purchase decision is perceived to be, the greater the percentage of informal verbal communication. Thus, important and/or complex decisions generate a greater amount of communication within the buying organization and the percent of this communication that is spoken (word-of-mouth) increased. Buying decisions that include a negotiation process also tend to have a lower percent of written communication $(r = -.26, p < .08)$. Negotiations tend to be spoken and only later confirmed by written contract. A negotiated purchase increases the total amount of communication within the buying organization. The higher the purchasing manager's position in the company, the longer he has worked for the company, and the more years of experience he has in purchasing for his company, the less his communications tend to be written $(r = -.26, p < .08; r = -.48, p < .01; r = -.37, p < .02,$ respectively).

The amount of written communications involved in buying decisions ranged from almost none to 100 percent. Some decisions involving additional contract work were 100 percent written between the buying company and the contractor under retainer, while others, such as the purchase of a 14-foot vertical boring mill, were accomplished entirely through verbal negotiations and oral contracts. For purchases involving capital equipment, the mean percent of written communication was 67. The median was 74 percent, indicating that the majority of communication in industrial buying of capital equipment tends to be written. Communication in the purchase of services had a mean of 60 percent written. The median was 51 percent. The percent of written communication in the purchase of services is lower than in the purchase of capital equipment.

Organizational Centralization

The purchasing function was organized in three different ways within the 31 companies studied in this research. Nine companies

operated in a completely decentralized manner with all purchasing
being done at the divisional- or separate-operating-location level.
An additional 10 companies operated in a semidecentralized manner
with some purchases being made at the divisional or plant level,
while others were made at the corporate level. In some cases the
requirement existed to inform the corporate purchasing department
of planned purchases so that the possibility of combining needs of different divisions could be considered in respect to reducing costs
through large-volume orders. Twelve companies bought all goods
and services entirely through a centralized corporate purchasing department. Purchasing departments in firms where the purchasing
function was centralized tended to be larger ($r = .25$, $p < .09$). Centralized purchasing departments also tended to impose dollar limits
on the purchasing personnel more often ($r = .25$, $p < .09$). Larger
companies, as measured by the number of employees, tended to be
more decentralized in their purchasing organization ($r = -.24$, $p < .09$).
Sales of companies had no significant effect on purchasing organization.

The purchasing departments involved in the specific purchases
examined by this study were located at the plant level, the divisional
level, and the corporate level. No significant difference can be detected between the level of the purchasing department involved in the
purchase of capital equipment and industrial services. Table 5.2
breaks down the purchases by department level.

The number of personnel employed as purchasing specialists
in the companies studied varied from 2 in the smallest purchasing
department, which consisted of only a purchasing agent and his secretary, to 200 in the largest purchasing department. The median
number of purchasing specialists was 10. Larger companies as mea-

TABLE 5.2

Level of Purchasing Departments by Buying Decisions

Purchasing Department Level	Purchase Category	
	Capital Equipment	Industrial Services
Plant	2	3
Division	13	12
Corporate	16	16

sured by both sales and number of employees had larger purchasing departments ($r = .44$, $p < .01$; $r = .38$, $p < .02$, respectively). The complexity of organizations also affected the size of the purchasing departments within the company. The greater the number of divisions and subsidiaries, the larger the purchasing department ($r = .37$, $p < .02$). The greater the number of separate operating locations and plants, the larger the purchasing department ($r = .50$, $p < .01$).

Purchase-Situation Attributes

The Importance of the Purchase Situations

The perceived importance of the purchase situation was measured using the average score of all buying-center members on a 10-point scale in response to the question, How important was this purchase compared with all the other purchases your company makes? One on the scale stood for "not at all important," while 10 stood for "of the utmost importance." The mean perceived importance of capital-equipment purchases was 7 and the median was 8. Services had a mean perceived importance of 6 while the median was 7. This should not be interpreted to indicate that capital-equipment purchases are as a class more important than the purchase of services. What is interesting is the distribution of the 62 purchase situations over the 10-point scale. While purchases of capital equipment tend to bunch at the important end of the scale, services are more evenly distributed over the scale in perceived importance. Figure 5.1 depicts the distribution of the perceived importance of both purchase classes. The bar charts appear to depict a situation where the majority of purchases of capital equipment are important, while perhaps indicating two categories of importance for services. The bimodal distribution of purchases in the industrial-services class seems to be quite different from the distribution depicted by the capital-equipment perceived-importance distribution.

The number of vendors involved in the buying decision was not significantly correlated ($r = .04$) to the importance of the purchase of capital equipment. The opposite was true for purchases in the industrial-services category. The more important the service was perceived to be, the greater the number of vendors involved in the process ($r = .28$, $p < .06$).

The purpose of the purchase (what the equipment or service was to be used for) was categorized as either primary or ancillary. A primary purchase was one that would be used directly in furthering the company's business function (that is, production or sales), while an ancillary purchase was one that was not directly involved in furthering the throughput or output processes of the company. Table 5.3

FIGURE 5.1

Perceived Importance of Purchases

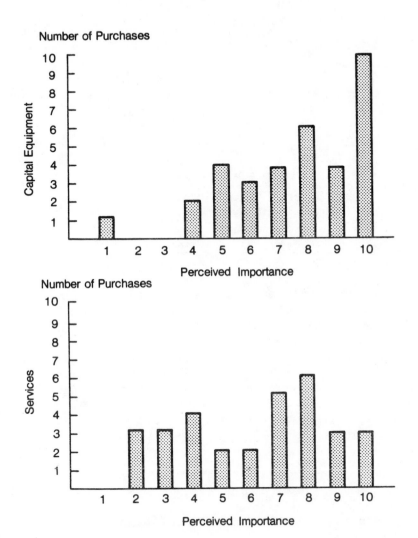

gives examples according to this typology and also the total sample count in each category. Primary purchases of both capital and industrial services were perceived as more important than ancillary purchases $(r = .31, p < .05; r = .69, p < .01,$ respectively).

The level in the company for which the capital equipment or service was purchased was noted. For purchases of capital equipment, 16 purchases were made for the plant level, 11 for the divi-

TABLE 5.3

Typology of Purchase Class by Involvement in Production

	Capital Equipment	Services
Primary	26 (83.9%) Automatic Drilling Machine Locomotive Crane Leveler Wrapping Machine	15 (48.4%) Tar Sludge Removal Machinery Rigging Labor Construction Contract Fabricating
Ancillary	4 (16.1%) Executive Office Desk Storage Shelving Stand By Heating System Gasoline Storage Tank	16 (51.6%) Typewriter Maintenance Drapery Cleaning Installation of Fire Prevention System Vending Machine Service

sional level, and 4 for the corporate. Services examined in the sample tended to be purchased more for the corporate level. Seven purchases in the industrial-services category were made for the plant level, and 12 for both the divisional and corporate level. There was no significant difference in perceived importance of capital equipment based upon the level for which they were purchased. Purchases of services, however, were viewed as more important the higher the level in the firm they were purchased for ($r = .27$, $p < .07$). Table 5.4 indicates the number of purchases made at each level for the two product categories.

TABLE 5.4

Company Levels for Which Purchases Were Made

	Capital Equipment	Services
Corporate	4	12
Division	11	12
Plant	16	7

TABLE 5.5

Highest Level of Management Involved in the Buying Center for the
Purchase Situations

	Capital Equipment	Services
Board of Directors	6	2
Top Management	16	13
Policy Level Manage-	2	3
Upper Operating Level	7	14
Total	31	31

The highest level of management involvement was also noted for each purchase. Six categories were defined. These were production/clerical worker, lower-level operating management, upper-level operating management, policy-setting-level management, top management, and board of directors and/or owner. There was no significant correlation between the perceived importance of a capital-equipment purchase and the level of management involved. There was, however, a significant relationship between these two variables when the purchase concerned an industrial service ($r = .43$, $p < .01$). Table 5.5 depicts the highest level of involvement in each of the 62 purchases studied. In all cases, levels of management from upper-operating management and above were involved in the decision-processes; that is, there were no cases in which levels of management of upper operating or above were not represented. Purchases of industrial services were more often made at lower levels in the management hierarchy than purchases of capital equipment.

Of the 31 purchases involving capital equipment, 24 involved a competitive-bidding procedure. Only 17 of the industrial-service purchases involved competitive bidding. Ten of the capital-equipment purchases involved negotiation between the buyer and seller, while 17 of the industrial-services purchases involved negotiation. There were a few situations in both product categories in which neither bidding nor negotiation took place, and the buyer simply paid the list or

TABLE 5.6

Pricing Method Used in the Purchase Situations

	Bid	Negotiated	Bid and Negotiated	Neither (Paid List Price)
Capital Equipment	18	4	6	3
Services	12	12	5	2

"asking" price. Table 5.6 illustrates the incidence of pricing methods for the 62 case studies.

The more important purchases of capital equipment and services tended to be negotiated ($r = .44$, $p < .01$ for capital equipment; $r = .24$, $p < .10$ for industrial services). Also, the larger the company, the more likely it was to negotiate a purchase than to seek competitive bids ($r = .48$, $p < .01$ and $r = .54$, $p < .001$ for capital equipment and $r = .39$, $p < .02$ and $r = .36$, $p < .025$ for industrial services).

The Complexity of the Purchase Situations

The perceived complexity of the purchase situation was measured using the average score of all buying-center members on a 10-point scale in response to the question, How complex or difficult to evaluate were the alternatives available for this purchase? One on the scale stood for "extremely simple and easy to evaluate." The mean perceived complexity for purchases of capital equipment was 6 and the median was also 6. Industrial services had a mean perceived complexity of 4 and the median was also 4.

Figure 5.2 depicts the distribution of the perceived complexity of both purchase classes. The bar charts illustrate a situation in which the majority of purchases of services are relatively easy to evaluate and only a few are above the midpoint of the scale. The distribution of the perceived complexity of the capital equipment appears to be bimodal with some types of purchases being relatively easy to evaluate and others extremely difficult.

Another measure of the complexity of the purchase situation was the number of vendors and offers involved. The number of vendors involved in the capital-equipment-purchase situations ranged from only 1 up to a high of 13 vendors involved in one particular situation.

FIGURE 5.2

Perceived Complexity of Purchases

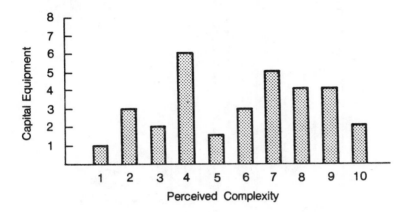

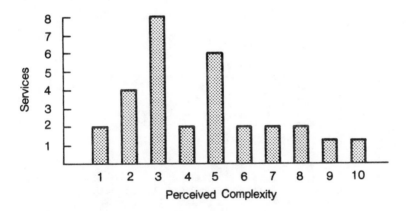

The number of vendors competing in the industrial-service situations ranged from one to eight. The mean number of vendors involved in the capital-equipment-purchase situations was four and the median was three. In the industrial-service situations, both the mean and median number of vendors was three. Figure 5.3 depicts the distribution of the number of vendors involved in the purchase situations.

As the charts indicate, it is only rarely that more than four vendors are involved in a purchase situation. The distributions for

FIGURE 5.3

Number of Vendors Involved in Purchases

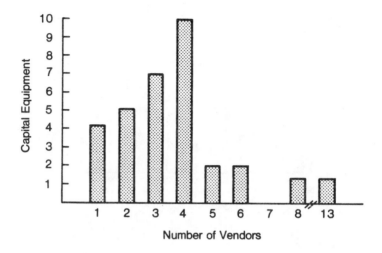

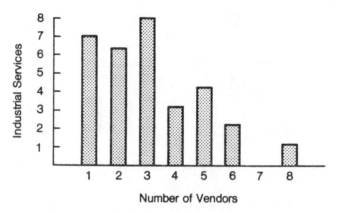

both purchase classes appear similar, with the exception that the number of vendors involved in purchase situations of services peaks at one less than those involved in capital-equipment-buying situations.

The time that it took to complete the entire buying process from first-recognized need to the purchase conclusion was another measure used to indicate the complexity of each purchase situation. The shortest time to complete a capital-equipment purchase was one week; the longest time period for capital equipment was two years. Services ranged from two weeks to seven and a half years in length of time to complete the entire purchase process. The mean length of time to complete a purchase of capital equipment was a little over six months (27 weeks); the median time period was 18 weeks.

Services on the average took less time to purchase. Perhaps this was due to a number of the service-purchase situations occurring on an annual basis and being completed in the last month of the yearly cycle. The mean time for completion of the purchase of services was slightly less than five months (20 weeks), while the median was 4 weeks. The amount of time required to complete a purchase decision correlated significantly with both the perceived importance and complexity of the purchase situation. For purchases of capital equipment, the more important the purchase, the longer the time involved to complete it ($r = .35$, $p < .025$). The same held true for services ($r = .30$, $p < .05$). The more complex the purchase situation was perceived to be, the longer it took to complete it ($r = .24$, $p < .09$ for capital-equipment purchases and $r = .49$, $p < .01$ for purchases of services). Thus the length of time to complete a purchase gives an indication of its complexity.

The Novelty of the Purchase Situations

If one were to use the typology of Robinson, Faris, and Wind (1967), the purchases in each product class could be categorized as new tasks, modified rebuys, and straight rebuys. Eight purchases of capital equipment and two of services were completely new tasks to the members of the respective firms. The largest number of purchases in each class were modified rebuys; 21 purchases of capital equipment and 19 of industrial services. Two purchases of capital equipment were straight rebuys, but a full 10 of industrial services fell into this category. This typology is interesting but may confound a number of separate dimensions such as the recency of a similar purchase, the importance of the purchase, and how many vendors were involved in the buying-decision process. For this reason, two other measures of the novelty of a purchase were developed.

The number of times a purchase was made during the course of a year was the first of these measures. Purchases of capital equipment tended to be made more often than those of services. Although the median for the number of times purchases similar to the ones in this sample were made during the course of a year was one for both capital equipment and services, the mean was about three times a month for capital equipment (34 times per year) and about once a month for services (15 times per year). Some purchases of capital equipment were made as often as every day. Other purchases of both capital equipment and services occurred less than once each year. Certain purchases had never occurred before, while others had occurred but so long in the past that no one currently with the particular firm had been involved with the purchase-decision process.

Another measure of the novelty of a purchase was the amount of time that had passed since the last time a similar purchase had been made. Some purchases of capital equipment had been made less than one week prior to the purchase under study, while one had not been made for over 35 years. Two purchases had never been made before. Services had also been purchased as recently as one week prior to the decision studied. One service had not been purchased for five years until the recent purchase of this service. One purchase of a service had never been made before.

The novelty of the purchase situation to the buying company had an effect on how a price for the service or piece of capital equipment was arrived at. Capital equipment that was more novel to the buying company was more often priced by negotiation ($r = .40$, $p < .02$). The pricing of more novel industrial services was accomplished through bidding procedures ($r = .62$, $p < .001$). This finding is somewhat counterintuitive in that, given the greater intangibility of services over capital equipment, it would seem logical for services, especially those that were purchased less often or were more novel to the buying firm, to be carefully negotiated. Also, because of the tangibility of capital equipment, bidding on a project would seem a more simple and exacting pricing method for the company that lacked experience in those types of purchases.

General Characteristics of the
Criterion (Dependent) Variables

Lateral Involvement in the
Industrial Buying Decision Process

The lateral dimension of the buying-center concept was operationalized as the number of separate departments, divisions, and functions involved in the purchase-decision/communication network. For purchases of capital equipment, the lateral involvement of different departments ranged from one for the narrowest purchase decision to eight for the broadest lateral-dimension purchase. The mean number of departments/functions involved in capital-equipment was four. The most commonly involved functions were purchasing, engineering, production, and sales/marketing. The median of departmental/functional involvement was also four. Services tended to have a slightly narrower lateral involvement. The horizontal influence within buying organizations ranged from only one department/function to six different lateral influences. The mean number of lateral-influencing departments/functions was three. The median was also three. The most commonly involved departments/functions were purchasing, production, and engineering.

Vertical Involvement in the
Industrial Buying-Decision Process

This structural dimension of the buying center primarily concerns hierarchical distribution of authority in buying-decision processes. The vertical involvement dimension was operationalized by identifying the various levels of management that became involved in the buying-decision communication network. In an effort to standardize this dimension across all 31 firms, six levels of hierarchical structure were identified and defined. These levels have previously been discussed and were labeled as board/owner; top management (president, executive vice-president, vice-president and general manager, group vice-president, and so on); policy-level management (functional vice-presidents); upper-level operating management (plant superintendents, managers of functional departments, sales managers); lower-level operating management (buyers, sales representatives, engineers); and clerical/worker employee level (secretaries, production workers).

For purchases of capital equipment, the minimum number of levels of the management hierarchy involved in the decision process was two. In some of the purchase situations, all six levels of the hierarchy were involved. This dimension can be referred to as the depth of the buying center. Vertical involvement in the purchase of services ranged from 1 to 5 levels of the management hierarchy. The mean number of levels involved in purchasing situations of capital equipment was three. For services, it was two levels.

This dimension in conjunction with the lateral-involvement dimension gives structure to the buying-center concept. By developing these dimensions, buying centers can be viewed as having depth and breadth of involvement by management and functional areas within the firm.

Extension of the Responsibilities
of the Buying-Center System

When the buying center is viewed as an organizational subsystem involved in information processing, two other dimensions can be defined and operationalized. These two dimensions are extension and connectedness; they are concerned with the group dynamics of the buying-decision communication process. The term extension refers to the total number of individuals involved in the buying center regardless of their departmental/functional or hierarchical position. The amount of extension of buying centers involved in the purchase of capital equipment ranged from 3 persons to 28. The mean number of individuals involved in the communication networks examined in this research was 8.

The extension of buying centers concerned with the purchase of services ranged from 2 to 15. The mean buying-center extension for service purchases was 5.

It is possible for two buying centers to have the same structural properties (lateral and vertical dimensions) yet be extended differently. The extension of the buying center is believed to be a function of the input load of information.

Connectedness of the Buying-Center System

The connectedness of the buying center was defined as the interconnection among the various participants. The actual number of dyads formed through formal and informal means of communication was compared with the total number of possible dyads that could have communicated with each other.

Connectedness ranged from 20 percent to 75 percent connectivity in groups involved with purchases of capital equipment. The mean percentage of connectivity in communication networks of buying centers of capital equipment was 45 percent.

The range of connectivity for buying centers involved in the purchase of services was greater than those of the capital-equipment communication networks. Connectedness ranged from 14 percent to 83 percent. Groups involved in the purchase of services tended to be more highly connected than those involved in the purchase of capital equipment. The mean connectedness of buying centers' purchasing services was 50 percent. All other things being equal, however, smaller groups tend to be better connected, because it is easier for members of a smaller group to communicate with everyone than it is for members of a larger group.

Connectedness is believed to be related to how quickly information can be disseminated within a group. The greater the connectedness of a group, the faster the information dissemination. Also, the greater the connectedness of a group, the greater the usage of prior information concerning the buying task.

The Centrality of the Purchasing Manager
in the Buying-Center System

The centrality of the purchasing manager was measured using matrix algebra and the communication matrixes developed for each case study. The purchasing manager's centrality varied to a great extent. The purchasing manager tended to be more central in the communication networks concerning the purchase of capital equipment but only slightly so.

Summary of the Findings concerning
the Sample's Basic Statistics

The companies that participated in the study are of medium-to-large size. Their complexity, as measured by the number of divisions, subsidiaries, and plants, ranges from simple to highly complex. Most of the companies are industrial manufacturers. The formalization of purchasing policies and procedures varies from relatively informal purchasing processes to highly formalized, carefully developed purchasing procedures. The organizations are centralized to varying degrees. This centralization seems interrelated with size and formalization.

The purchases examined by this research fall into two prespecified categories—capital equipment and industrial services. The importance of the purchases varies to a great extent. Purchases of capital equipment in this study as a whole seemed to be perceived as more important than the services studied as purchases. It is perhaps wise not to draw too serious a conclusion from this comparison, for although participants were asked to identify a recent purchase in each category, response biases could be operating. Primary and ancillary purchases were identified and examined. Purchases of a primary nature (directly involved in the production or sales function) were perceived as significantly more important than ancillary purchases. The complexity of the purchase situations varied sufficiently across this dimension to capture buying decisions involving situations of all levels of complexity. Differing levels of purchase-situation novelty were also examined. To use the familiar typology of the BUYGRID, there were 10 new-task situations, 40 modified rebuys, and 12 straight rebuys. Methods of pricing used in the case studies were noted and interesting relationships were found concerning the effect novelty has on the method of pricing the product or service.

Finally, five new, dependent variables were defined and operationalized: lateral involvement, vertical involvement, extension, connectedness, and the centrality of the purchasing specialist in the communication network. Lateral and vertical involvement are structural variables of depth and breadth in the buying-center concept. Extension and connectedness view the buying center as a dynamic, dyadic system for information processing. The centrality of the purchasing specialist views the status of the purchasing function in this dyadic system of communication using sociometric techniques. All

TABLE 5.7

Concepts and Measurements by Firms/Purchase Situations/ Purchasing Managers Matrix

Concepts and (Measurement)	Firm/Purchase Situation/Purchasing Manager

Organizational Structure
Size
  (Sales in Dollars--SALES)
  (Number of Employees--
    EMP)
 	
Complexity
  (Number of Divisions/
    Subsidiaries--DIVSUB)
  (Number of Plants--
    PLANTS)
 	
Formalization
  (Does a Purchasing Manual
    Exist--MANUAL)
  (Do Dollars Authorization
    Limits Exist--LIMIT$)
  (Perceived Formalization
    --FORMAL)
  (Percentage of Communica-
    tion Written--WRITEN)
 	
Centralization
  (Purchasing Function
    Organization--PUROG)
	1 2 3 31

Purchase Situation Attributes
Importance
  (Perceived Importance--
    IMPORT)
  (Purpose, Primary/Ancil-
    lary--PRIMARY)
 	
Complexity
  (Perceived Complexity--
    COMPLEX)
  (Numbef of Vendors In-
    volved--VENDORS)
  (Time Acquired to Complete
    Purchase--TIME)
 	
Novelty
  (Buygrid Categorization--
    NEWNESS)
  (Last Time Purchase Was
    Made--LASTIME)
  (How Many Times Per Year Is
    the Purchase Made—OFTEN)
	Firm 1 . . . Firm 31
	Capital Equipment/... ...Capital Equip-
	    Service ment/Service

Characteristics of
  Purchasing Managers
 	
(Purchasing Managers
  Position--PMPOS)
(Certified as Purchasing
  Manager--CPM)
(How Long Worked for
  Company--WKCO)
(How Long Worked for
  Company in Pur-
  chasing--WKPURCO)
(Total Years Experience
  in Purchasing--TOTYRSP)
(Level of Education--
  EDUC)
(Number of People in
  Your Department--
  NUMPPL)
(Your Department's Level
  in the Company--
  DPTLEV)
	Firm 1 Capital Equip- ... Firm 31
	  ment/Service
	
	PM--Firm 1, PM Firm 1 ... PM--Firm 31
	  CE Service CE etc.

variables seemed sufficiently conceived and varied enough to permit empirical analysis. This was accomplished using stepwise linear regression and is discussed in the next section of this chapter.

Table 5.7 presents the theoretical concepts believed to have effects on the dimensions of the buying-center system and the measures used to operationalize these concepts. Each firm, purchase situation, or purchasing manager involved were measured on these variables.

ANALYSIS OF THE BUYING CENTER'S DIMENSIONS AND THE CENTRALITY OF THE PURCHASING MANAGER USING STEPWISE LINEAR REGRESSION

Multiple regression was viewed as an appropriate technique through which to analyze the relationship between the dependent or criterion variables and the set of independent or predictor variables and thereby test the hypotheses developed in Chapter 3.

Results of the Stepwise-Linear-Regression Analysis

In all, 12 regression equations were constructed. Equations for each criterion variable were constructed for both types of purchase classes (capital equipment and industrial services) using the structural variables of the firm and purchase-situation attributes as predictor variables. In addition, two equations—one for each purchase class—were constructed attempting to explain the centrality of the purchasing manager in the communication network as a function of the characteristics of the purchasing manager. Appendix 2 contains tables summarizing the findings of all 12 regression equations.

Tables 5.8 and 5.9 present the equations with appropriate statistics. The regression coefficients in Tables 5.8 and 5.9 have been computed on standardized X and Y values rather than on the original values. These standardized regression coefficients are referred to as "beta weights." When both X and Y variables are standardized, the Y intercept becomes zero. Thus, there is no constant included in the regression equation.

Examining Capital-Equipment Purchases through Linear Regression

Explaining Lateral Involvement in the Buying Center. Lateral involvement in the buying center, or the number of different departments/functions and divisions within a company participating in the

TABLE 5.8

Capital-Equipment Regression Equations

Dependent Variable	$\bar{R}^2$	Independent Variables/Beta Weight Coefficients and Significance	Regression F Ratio	P<
Vertical Involvement	.58	.45 IMPORT** - .52 LIMIT$** - .31 FORMAL* + .26 DIVSUB + .36 PURORG* - .24 OFTEN + .26 VENDORS	6.73	.01
Lateral Involvement	.32	.23 IMPORT + .42 EMP* - .32 DIVSUB - .23 OFTEN + .34 WRITEN + .25 NEWNESS - .18 PLANTS	2.91	.05
Extension	.53	.48 IMPORT** - .28 LIMIT$ - .29 OFTEN* - .17 MANUAL + .32 SALES + .19 PRIMARY - .22 FORMAL - .18 PLANTS	5.03	.01
Connectedness	.52	-.52 WRITEN** - .53 MANUAL** - .43 (Number of Individuals in the Buying Center) + .34 SALES* + .29 VENDORS + .23 PURORG*		
Purchasing Manager's Centrality (PMC)	.14	.37 VENDORS* - .32 PRIMARY	3.35	.05
Purchasing Manager's Centrality (PMC)--Regressed Against the characteristics of the PM	.05	-.23 NUMPPL + .26 CPM - .18 WKCO	1.49	>.10

**p < .01
*p < .05

TABLE 5.9

Industrial-Services Regression Equations

Dependent Variable	$\bar{R}^2$	Independent Variables/Beta Weight Coefficients and Significance	Regression F Ratio	P<
Vertical Involvement	.62	.33 TIME + .26 IMPORT + .30 PLANTS + .34 PURORG** - .34 FORMAL + .31 SALES + .24 LASTIME*	7.71	.01
Lateral Involvement	.48	.23 NEWNESS + .47 TIME + .44 DIVSUB - .22 FORMAL** + .38 WRITEN + .34 LASTIME - .49 PRIMARY + .42 IMPORT* - .22 MANUAL	4.00	.01
Extension	.73	.50 TIME + .22 IMPORT + .46 EMP - .44 FORMAL** + .32 VENDORS + .16 LASTIME**	13.80	.01
Connectedness	.57	-.69 (Number of Individuals in the Buying Center)** + .36 VENDORS + .23 PRIMARY - .30 OFTEN - .19 MANUAL* + .17 PURORG	6.50	.01
Purchasing Manager's Centrality (PMC)	.17	.53 LIMITS - .33 TIME - .51 IMPORT + .33 COMPLEX + .25 PRIMARY*	2.21	.10
Purchasing Manager's Centrality (PMC) --Regressed against the characteristics of the PM	.46	.52 CPM - .17 PMPOS + .48 TOTYRSP - .29 DPTLEV** - .30 WKCO*	6.01	.01

**p < .01
*p < .05

117

buying center, was found to be best explained using seven of the independent variables. Approximately 32 percent of the variance was explained ($\overline{R}^2$ = .32) and the regression-equation F-ratio was significant at $p < .05$.

The perceived importance of the purchase situation was the variable that explained the greatest amount of variance in lateral involvement and entered the equation first. As hypothesized, the relationship between the two variables was positively correlated. The size of the company as measured by the number of employees the company employed also had a positive effect on lateral involvement. Organizational complexity, as measured by the number of divisions and subsidiaries as well as the number of plants a company was divided into, was found to negatively affect the extent of lateral involvement. This finding was counter to the original hypothesis and leaves room for post hoc speculation concerning the reason for this effect. The novelty of a purchase, measured by the newness of the purchase situation and the number of times (OFTEN) a purchase was made within a year's time, was found to increase the extent of lateral involvement, as hypothesized. Finally, lateral involvement was noted to be positively affected by the extent to which communication was written. In conclusion, it can be seen that lateral involvement in the buying center is affected by both structural variables of the firm and purchase-situation attributes. Only the F-ratio of one variable was significant above an α level of .05. It should be remembered that independent variables were added to the regression equation as long as their F-ratio was above 1.0 and the adjusted R^2 was increased by their addition.

Explaining Vertical Involvement in the Buying Center. Vertical involvement, operationalized as the number of different levels of the management hierarchy involved in the buying-decision process, was also found to be most affected by the perceived importance of the purchase situation. The greater the perceived importance of the purchase situation, the more levels of the management hierarchy there are involved in the purchase process. Formalization of purchasing policies and procedures, especially limiting the amount of dollars various ranks are authorized to commit, severely lowers the involvement of different levels of the management structure. This is perhaps due to only those levels that are required to be involved in the process being involved. The greater the centralization of authority, the greater the amount of vertical involvement that was found. If a need were identified at a relatively lower level in a highly centralized organization, it would have to rise through all the levels between the level where the need was identified and the level with the necessary authority to approve the purchase. Thus, a greater number

of levels of management were involved when the organization was
more formalized than less formalized. Other variables that entered
the equation were the number of divisions and subsidiaries (DIVSUB),
the number of vendors involved in the purchase (VENDORS), and how
often the purchase was made within a year's time. The beta weight
coefficients for these variables were not significant, however.

Explaining Buying-Center Extension. Again, the variable found to
have the greatest effect on the buying-center extension was the perceived importance of the purchase situation. The greater the importance of the purchase situation, the greater the number of people
involved in the purchasing process. This relationship was especially
true when the purchase was to be used directly in the production or
marketing process of the firm (PRIMARY). The only other purchase-
situation attribute to enter the equation was how often the purchase
occurred. The more often a purchase occurred, or perhaps the more
routine a purchase was, the less the number of people involved in the
buying-center system.

Organizational size, formalization, and complexity also had
effects on the extension of the buying center. The size of the organization increased the number of people involved in the buying-decision process. This is probably due to responsibilities within the organization being more divided, and, thus, any particular task simply
requires the efforts of more people. Formalization of purchasing
procedures and policies had a limiting effect on individuals entering
the buying center. The perceived formality of the process, the existence of a manual on purchasing procedures, and limits on dollar-
authorization levels all had clearly negative effects on buying-center
extension.

The complexity of the organization, as measured by the number
of separate operating locations and number of plants, had a negative
effect on the buying-center extension. This was the only variable
entering the equation that exhibited an effect in the opposite direction
from that hypothesized. It could be that individuals in more complex
organizations have less overall interest in becoming involved in
tasks unless it is absolutely necessary that they do so. Buying-center
extension is a measure of both the informal involvement and formal
influence of people within the firm on the buying-decision process.
Organizational complexity had a negative effect on lateral involvement but a positive effect on vertical involvement. The overall effect
on the number of people involved is negative, however.

Explaining Buying-Center Connectedness. Connectedness, defined
as the amount of interconnection among the individuals involved in
the buying center, was found to be very negatively affected by the

existence of a purchasing-procedures manual and the extent to which the communication of the buying process was written. Buying decisions that were primarily written followed a very linear (from one person to the next) path and, therefore, limited the interconnectedness of the buying center. An additional variable was added to this regression. Because it was known that the number of people in a group affect that group's interconnectedness, the variable measuring the number of people involved in the buying center was also regressed for its effect. As expected, this variable had a significant negative effect on buying-center connectedness. Size of the company, as measured by sales, had a significant effect on buying-center connectedness but in the opposite direction from that hypothesized. The larger the company, the greater the buying center's connectedness. The degree of centralization of the purchasing function, as expected, had a positive effect on connectedness.

The complexity of the purchasing situation, as measured by the number of vendors involved in the buying decision, had a positive effect on buying-center participants' interconnectedness.

Explaining the Purchasing Manager's Centrality in Purchases of
Capital Equipment. This is the regression analysis in which the least success was attained. Only two variables entered the equation with F-ratios above 1.0. Of these, only one was statistically significant. While the equation's F-ratio was significant at $p < .05$, the amount of explained variance was only 14 percent ($\bar{R}^2 = .14$).

The number of vendors involved in the purchasing situation has a significant positive effect on the centrality of the purchasing manager. The more vendors involved, the more central the purchasing specialist is in the communication network. This makes intuitive sense if the purchasing specialist is the interface between his company and vendors in the purchasing. This is the case, as will be seen in the next section when the aggregate communication matrixes are examined. It seems that there may be two types of purchase-situation complexity, then. One type would be related to the number of vendors and difference in product offerings, while the other type of complexity would be related to technical evaluation of the company's needs and matching the desired product. Purchase-situation complexity is a variable that appears to need greater examination.

If the capital equipment is of a primary nature to the buying organization, the purchasing manager's centrality to the process is reduced. Production and engineering probably become more central on these types of purchases.

In addition to examining the purchasing manager's centrality in the buying center as a function of the structural variables of the firm and the purchase-situation attributes, individual characteristics and differences among the purchasing managers were used as predictor variables to explain differences in centrality in the buying center. In the capital-equipment-purchase situations, this regression met with no success. The equation's F-ratio was not significant below the $p < .10$ level. None of the variables that entered the equation were significant. Only about 5 percent of the variance was explained.

Examining Industrial-Service Purchases through Linear Regression

Explaining Lateral Involvement in the Buying Center. Lateral involvement was most affected by the complexity of the purchase situation as measured by the time it took to complete the purchase and the complexity of the organization as measured by the number of divisions and subsidiaries of the organization. The novelty of the purchase and the amount of communication in writing also had positive effects on the extent of lateral involvement in the purchasing process. If the service was to be directly involved in the firm's primary operations, the extent of lateral involvement was significantly limited. Perceived formality and a manual of purchasing policies and procedures limited lateral involvement.

Explaining Vertical Involvement in the Buying Center. Both structural variables of the firm and purchase-situation attributes had highly significant effects on vertical involvement in the buying-decision process. The time that it took to accomplish a purchase had a positive effect on vertical involvement. The longer it took, the greater vertical involvement in the process. Therefore, the more complex a purchase situation of services is, the greater the number of levels of management that get involved. The more centralized an organization, the greater the vertical involvement. While the relationship between the complexity of a purchase and the degree of lateral involvement was not the one hypothesized, the relationship between organizational centralization and vertical involvement is in the direction hypothesized.

The perceived formalization of buying policies was also significantly correlated in a negative manner with vertical involvement. This was as hypothesized.

Explaining Buying-Center Extension. Again, time was the variable with a major effect on the buying center. The time that it took to complete a purchase of a service was the best prediction of how many people would be involved in the buying center. The longer the time required, the greater the number of people involved in the buying center. The size of the company, as measured by the number of employees, also had a positive effect on the buying-center extension.

However, the more formal the purchasing process was perceived to be, the less people were involved in the buying center. Purchase-situation attributes that also had positive effects on buying-center extension were the perceived importance of the purchase, the number of vendors involved, and the novelty of the purchase for the buying company.

A very high percentage of variance in buying-center extension was explained by only six predictor variables ($R^2 = .73$). This was the regression equation with the greatest explanatory power of all 12 equations. Three variables (the time it took to complete the purchase, the number of employees of the firm, and the perceived formalization of buying policies and procedures) were highly significant in explaining buying-center extension ($p < .01$).

Explaining Buying-Center Connectedness. As expected, the number of people involved in the buying-center purchasing process had a main influence on the connectedness of the buying center. The more people there were, the lower was the connectedness of the buying center. Formalization of purchasing policies through the use of a manual lowered connectedness, as did the amount of communication that was written versus spoken. Centralization of the firm's purchasing function had an increasing effect on buying-center connectedness.

Purchase-situation attributes also had effects on the connectedness of the buying center. The number of vendors involved had a positive effect; the more vendors involved, the greater the connectedness of the buying center. This was expected; a normal reaction to increased complexity of the buying situation is to increase buying-center connectedness. If the purchase was of a primary nature, buying-center connectedness was also increased. Finally, the novelty of a purchase of service increased the amount of interconnectedness between buying-center participants.

Explaining the Purchasing Manager's Centrality in Purchasing of Industrial Services. The attempt to explain the purchasing manager's centrality in the buying-center communication network through the use of structural variables of the firm and purchase-situation attributes was not much more successful for services than for capital equipment. Five independent variables entered the equation with F-ratios greater than 1. However, one one of the variables, regression coefficients were significant (LIMIT\$, $p < .01$). Approximately 17 percent of the variance of the purchasing manager's centrality could be explained using the variables.

An interesting turn of events occurred, however, when the characteristics of the purchasing manager were used to explain centrality.

A regression equation with an F-ratio with a significance of $p < .01$ was constructed. This equation explained 46 percent of the variance in the centrality of the purchasing manager in the communication network. The characteristic of the purchasing manager that had the greatest effect was whether the purchasing manager was certified or not. A certified purchasing manager (CPM) played a much more central role in purchases of services than did those not certified. The CPM qualification is a composite of a number of characteristics about the purchasing manager including experience, education, professional activity, and so on. It may also reflect the individual's firm's emphasis on purchasing specialization and professionalism. The CPM recognition is also a mark of achievement. This variable alone explained 30 percent of the variance of the dependent variable.

Other characteristics of the purchasing manager that entered the equation were the total years of purchasing experience the individual had, his position in the managerial hierarchy, the level of the purchasing department in the firm, and how long the individual had worked for the buying organization. Surprisingly, not all of these variables had positive effects on the purchasing manager's centrality. The higher the level of the purchasing department in the company, the lower the individual's centrality. Also, the higher the individual's position and the more years of experience with the company, the less central was the individual to the purchasing process. The results of this regression analysis indicate that for certain purchase classes (that is, services), individual differences in purchasing managers do make a difference. While studying the purchasing manager is itself insufficient to understand industrial buying behavior, if there are certain situations where the influence of the purchasing manager must be taken into account, understanding the purchasing manager is essential.

Comparison of the Results of the Regression Analysis

The results of the regression analysis of the two purchase classes provide interesting similarities and contrasts. With only one exception, all of the beta-weight coefficient signs were the same for an independent variable entering an equation, whether the purchase class was capital equipment or services. The exception was the number of divisions and subsidiaries of a company and the effect this variable had on lateral involvement. In the capital-equipment-purchase situations, the variable had a negative effect, while in the case of services it had a positive effect.

In each set of the four equations concerning the dimensions of the buying center, variables of structural aspects of the firm and purchase-situation attributes explained variance in the dependent variables. Overall, the amount of variance explained by the stepwise-linear-regression procedures was higher for the industrial-service-purchase situations. The significance of the F-ratio of the equations was not systematically higher for either set of purchase-class cases.

While quite a few variables appear in the corresponding equations for the two purchase classes, there are some interesting differences between those independent variables that explain variation in the dependent variables. In the capital-equipment-purchase situations, the perceived importance of the purchase situation has the greatest effect on lateral involvement, vertical involvement, and the overall number of people involved in the buying-center extension. In the cases concerned with industrial services, however, the length of time required to complete the purchase transaction had the greatest effect on lateral, vertical, and overall involvement in the buying center. The equations of buying-center connectedness are highly similar for the two purchase classes. The only differences in the two are that size of the company makes a difference in purchases of capital equipment, and purchase-situation attributes (PRIMARY and OFTEN) make a difference in purchases of services.

Of the four equations attempting to explain the centrality of the purchasing manager in the buying-center communication network, only the one using the individual characteristics of the purchasing manager and examining purchases of services could be called successful. It appears that, although an interesting concept, the centrality of an individual in a communication network needs further work to better explain this concept.

Hypothesis Testing of All Relationships

Because stepwise linear regression seeks parsimony in variables and maximum-explained variance, it does not provide a useful tool for testing all of the proposed hypotheses. Those independent variables that are highly correlated with other independent variables already in the regression equation may not be selected to enter the equation. An example of this would be the variable SALES not entering an equation in which EMP had already entered because the two variables are highly correlated with each other; there would probably also be little unexplained variance in the dependent variable that could be explained by the entry of SALES into the equation. For this reason, it is useful to examine the partial correlations between the dependent and independent variables to test the basic hypotheses for all the conceptual relationships postulated in Chapter 3. Appendix 3 presents the partial correlations between the criterion and predictor variables along with the hypothesized relationship. In

TABLE 5.10

Results of Hypothesis Tests for Capital-Equipment Purchases

	Structural Variables of the Firm				Purchase Situation Attributes		
	Size	Complexity	Formalization	Centralization	Importance	Novelty	Complexity
Vertical Involvement	- NS	- NS	- p<.01	+ p<.10	+ p<.01	+ p<.10	- NS
Lateral Involvement	+ p<.10	+ NS	? NS	- NS	+ NS	+ NS	+ NS
Extension	+ NS	+ NS	? correlation neg. p<.05	- NS	+ p<.05	+ p<.05	+ NS
Connectedness	- p<.05 oppos.	- p<.10	? correlation neg. p<.05	+ NS	+ p<.10 opposite direct.	+ p<.05	+ p<.01
Centrality (status) of Purchasing	+ NS	+ NS	? NS	? NS	- NS	- opposite direction p<.10	- opposite direction p<.10

Hypothesized Relationships Between the Criterion Variables and the Predictor Variables

Legend

+ Positive Correlation
- Negative Correlation
? Effect uncertain

Actual Relationships Between Variables

Legend

NS--no significant relationship
Opposite Direction--hypothesis was not supported, however a significant effect in opposite (from hypothesized direction) was noted.
p<--indicated hypothesis supported and level

constructing these partial correlations, the effect of other independent variables has been controlled, with the exception of those variables hypothesized to measure the same concept. In other words, for the partial correlation between lateral involvement and SALES, all independent variables have been controlled except EMP. Controlling for the effect of EMP would remove much of the variance explained by SALES. (Both variables are hypothesized to measure the concept of organizational size and are actually highly correlated, $r = .92^+$.)

Tables 5.10 and 5.11 summarize the findings of the partial correlations with regard to the hypotheses outlined in Chapter 3.

Clearly, not all of the hypotheses were supported. In many cases the correlations were in the predicted direction but simply just not strong enough. In other cases, the results were unclear because

TABLE 5.11

Results of Hypothesis Tests for Industrial-Services Purchases

	Structural Variables of the Firm				Purchase Situation Attributes		
	Size	Complexity	Formalization	Centralization	Importance	Novelty	Complexity
Vertical Involvement	- Op.Dir p<.10	- Opposite Dir p<.001	- p<.05	+ p<.01	+ NS	+ p<.05	- Rela. Unclear
Lateral Involvement	+ NS	+ p<.05	? Relationship Unclear	- NS	+ NS	+ p<.10	+ p<.01
Extension	+ p<.01	+ NS	? Relationship Unclear	- NS	+ NS	+ p<.05	+ p<.01
Connectedness	- NS	- NS	? Correlation Negative p<.10	+ NS	+ NS	+ p<.05	+ NS
Centrality (status) of Purchasing	+ NS	+ NS	? Correlation Positive p<.05	? NS	- NS	- NS	- NS

Hypothesized Relationships Between the Criterion Variables and the Predictor Variables

Legend

+ Positive Correlation

- Negative Correlation

? Effect Uncertain

Actual Relationships Between Variables--Legend
NS--no significant relationship
Opposite Direction--hypothesis was not supported however a significant effect in opposite (from hypothesized) direction was noted
p<--indicated hypothesis supported and level

of two or more variables purported to measure the same concept being significantly correlated with the dependent variable but in opposite directions. Finally, there were some relationships that were significantly correlated but in the opposite direction from those hypothesized.

It may also be noted that these partial correlations provide somewhat different results than were obtained by the regression analysis. This can be explained by when a variable is entered into the analysis. In the case of stepwise regression analysis, all independent variables are examined for correlation with the unexplained variance in the dependent variable, and that variable that is the most highly correlated enters the equation. With partial correlation, the effect of all other variables on the dependent is controlled for, or statistically removed, and then the independent variable under examination is entered into the analysis.

To put these various statistical techniques into better perspective, it is necessary to examine the findings of this research from an in-depth, qualitative perspective. The next three sections examine participation in and the process of industrial-buying situations.

PARTICIPATION AND COMMUNICATION IN INDUSTRIAL BUYING BEHAVIOR

This section aggregates the communication networks of each company into two composite matrixes, one for capital-equipment purchases and one for industrial-service purchases. The aggregate matrixes are composed of the communication dyads among the eight most frequently involved functional areas within a firm; a group of others, including those individuals within the firm not included in the eight most frequently involved functions and others outside the firm; and the vendors.

Figures 5.4 and 5.5 present the aggregate interaction matrixes for the 10 categories of buying-center participants.

The main diagonal of each matrix presents the amount of involvement of each function in the 31 cases for each product class. Only the vendor function was involved in every purchase situation. The reason for this was that only purchases that had taken place were studied, and, therefore, there always had to have been a seller. Future research may be directed at examining evolving purchase decisions, and some of these will probably not end in sales; but that type of study was beyond the scope of this research.

The cells not on the main diagonal indicate the extent to which communication took place between the row and column functions that intersect at that cell. Raw cell counts and percentages are provided in Appendix 4. Figures 5.4 and 5.5 provide only an indication if the communication between the functions occurred more or less frequently than probability would predict. The calculation for the dyad formation based upon probability was determined by the percent of participation of the row and column functions and the assumption that if two functions were represented in the buying center, there was a 50 percent chance (random) that they would communicate with each other; that is, the two frequencies of participation were multiplied together, giving the joint probability that both functions would be represented in any given buying center. (It was assumed that participation of functions was independent of the participation of other functions.) The joint probability of participation was then multiplied by .50 (giving the two functions a 50 percent chance of communicating), arriving at the expected probability that these two functions would communicate in the direction indicated. The actual probability that two functions

FIGURE 5.4

Summative Communication-Network Matrix of Capital-Equipment Purchases

Function	Purchasing	Engineering	MFG/Prod.	Acct/Finance	Sales/Marketing	Top Mgt.	Board/Owner	Shipping/Receiving	Others	Vendors
Purchasing	.97	+	+	-	-	-	-	+	+	+
Engineering	+	.65	+	-	Ø	-	-	-	+	Ø
MFG/Prod.	+	+	.74	Ø	+	+	-	-	+	-
Acct/Finance	+	-	Ø	.26	Ø	+	+	Ø	-	-
Sales/Mktg.	-	-	+	Ø	.32	+	-	-	+	-
Top Mgt.	-	-	+	+	Ø	.65	+	-	-	-
Board/Owner	-	Ø	Ø	+	-	Ø	.19	-	-	-
Shipping/Receiving	Ø	Ø	-	Ø	-	-	-	.26	Ø	-
Others	Ø	+	+	-	+	-	-	-	.55	-
Vendors	+	Ø	-	-	-	-	-	Ø	Ø	1.0

SENDS

RECEIVES

Cells on Main Diagonal = Frequency of involvement
Cells off Main Diagonal = Dyad formation (communication)
 Ø as probability predicts
 + greater than probability predicts
 - less than probability predicts

would communicate if they were both present in the buying center was .45 for capital-equipment purchases and .50 for service purchases based upon the mean integrative complexity of the respective buying centers. The number of dyads predicted by probability estimates was then compared with the number of dyads actually formed.

FIGURE 5.5

Summative Communication-Network Matrix of Industrial-Service
Purchases

Function	Purchasing	Engineering	Mfg/Prod.	Acct/Finance	Sales/Marketing	Top Mgt.	Board/Owner	Maintenance Services	Others	Vendors	
Purchasing	.90	+	+	–	–	–	–	–	+	+	
Engineering	+	.35	+	∅	–	–	∅	+	+	+	
Mfg/Prod.	+	+	.52	+	∅	+	∅	∅	+	–	
Acct/Finance	–	–	∅	.13	∅	+	∅	–	–	–	S
Sales/Mktg.	∅	–	∅	∅	.16	+	∅	∅	+	∅	E N D
Top Mgt.	–	–	+	+	+	.48	+	∅	+	–	S
Board/Owner	∅	∅	∅	∅	∅	+	.06	∅	∅	–	
Maintenance Services	+	+	∅	–	∅	∅	∅	.26	–	–	
Others	+	+	∅	–	+	+	∅	–	.42	∅	
Vendors	+	+	–	–	∅	–	–	–	+	1.0	

RECEIVES

Cells on Main Diagonal = Frequency of involvement

Cells off Main Diagonal = Dyad formation (communication)

∅ as probability predicts

+ greater than probability predicts

– less than probability predicts

A 10 percent (plus and minus) range around the number predicted by probability was used to compare with the actual number of dyads formed. This provided a range outside of which the communication between parties seemed noticeably different from chance. Each off-diagonal cell indicates whether the amount of actual dyad formation exceeded the predicted or not. By examining these cells, interesting patterns of interaction can be observed.

From a marketing-management perspective, the grand communication-network matrix is a useful tool in several ways. First, it helps the marketing manager to better understand how the buying center is structured. Second, it permits the manager to examine who vendors contact and who they might potentially gain an advantage by contacting. Finally, it provides the basis for developing advertising campaigns based upon reaching those individuals in the buying center whose participation is high but might not be reachable by personal sales calls (finance, top management, and so on).

A closer examination of the two matrixes will enable the further development of these proposed uses for the technique.

Participation and Communication
in Capital-Equipment Purchases

In addition to the presence of a vendor or vendors in each purchase of capital equipment, certain functions within the firm were usually involved in the buying process. The functions within the firm that were most often involved included purchasing, manufacturing or production, engineering, and top management. These functions could be said to be the nucleus of the buying center for capital-equipment purchases. Other functions regularly involved in the buying center included accounting and finance, sales and marketing, shipping and receiving, and the board of directors or the owner of the company. These functions were not involved in the majority of cases, however. Functions within the firm that had infrequent involvement and were included in the "others" category were safety, industrial engineering, maintenance, personnel, quality assurance, inventory control, and projects.

Others outside the firm were involved in 6 of the 31 cases. This word of mouth between other firms is important but does not seem to occur that often. It is something, however, that a marketing manager needs to be concerned with. The individuals outside the firm involved in the six purchase situations of capital equipment were a purchasing manager in another firm and two managers of production in other firms; three times a customer of the buying firm had an influence on the buying process. The participation of these functions were limited to either the opinion giving of a third party or, in the case of customers, involved often generating the recognition of the need for the purchase. That is, in the three cases in which the customer of a firm was involved, it was either to request a product or service that the company could only provide by purchasing the necessary capital equipment or to inform the company that they would be increasing their needs, thus requiring the purchase of additional manufacturing equipment.

The participation of the various functions is only part of the picture, however. What must also be taken into consideration besides simple participation in the buying-decision process is the pattern of communication between the various functions. Looking at the grand communication network, several interesting factors about the overall interaction of the buying center emerge. Purchasing, engineering, and manufacturing interact with each other quite heavily. Only purchasing and engineering interact with the vendor to any extent, while only manufacturing interacts heavily with top management. This pattern would seem to indicate several things: (1) engineering, purchasing, and manufacturing are really the center of the buying process for capital equipment; (2) purchasing and, to some extent, engineering have the role of interfacing with the vendors; and (3) manufacturing has the role of interfacing with top management.

Other functions such as accounting and finance, sales and marketing, and shipping and receiving play more minor, supporting roles. The role of accounting and finance seems to be to advise top management and the board of directors on especially important or financially complex purchases and to inform purchasing of which offer is the most financially appealing. Sales and marketing's role is to interface between the customer and production and top management. Sales and marketing have little interaction with purchasing. When the board of directors is involved, which is only for purchases of the utmost importance, or when the direction of the company is being changed and purchases of capital equipment are concomitant, they normally interact with top management and accounting and finance, although the board may seek input from engineering and manufacturing.

Top management is involved in the majority of capital-equipment purchases. The role of top management was often that of decider or arbitrator in cases where purchasing, engineering, and production could not come up with a unanimous recommendation on the offers. Top management communicated more often with manufacturing, accounting and finance, and the board of directors. Shipping and receiving most often received communication from purchasing, usually concerning the expected delivery of the equipment. Shipping and receiving only initiated communication when either the equipment arrived or was past due on delivery. These communications were directed to purchasing and engineering, accounting and finance, or others in the firm. The reason for contacting purchasing or engineering was to have them contact the vendor, something that shipping and receiving rarely did. The reason for contacting accounting and finance

FIGURE 5.6

The Probable Buying Center for Capital-Equipment Purchases

The Probable Buying Center for Capital Equipment

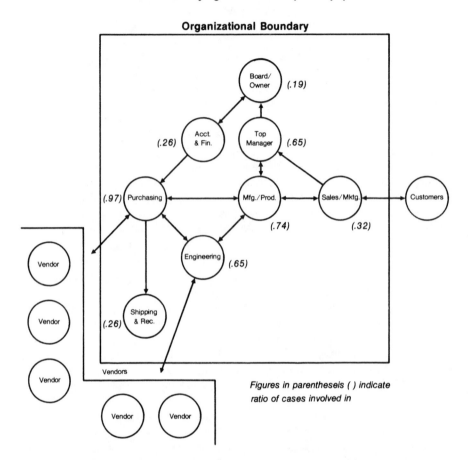

was to ensure payment, something that was often held up until the equipment was received and inspected. The reason for contacting others was that they were sometimes the user of the equipment.

The role of other functions not captured in the eight most-involved categories varied to a large extent. Safety was sometimes involved for inspection of installation. Industrial engineering often served as internal consultants to production and manufacturing. Projects became involved when the purchase was required because of a customer order. Projects were usually connected with sales and marketing.

The most interesting finding concerns the communication between the vendors and the buying company. In the 31 case studies reported here, this interaction was normally only between the vendor and purchasing and engineering. It would seem logical for vendors to try to contact both manufacturing and top management as well. While the system may be set up to prevent vendor communication with others in the firm besides purchasing and engineering, advertising can serve as a replacement for the direct-sales call on these functions. It may be, however, that many vendors are simply unaware of who is involved in the buying center and how the buying center functions. Figure 5.6 constructs the typical buying-center structure for the purchase of capital equipment based upon the flows of communication.

Participation and Communication
in Industrial-Service Purchases

The same functions that were involved in the purchase of capital equipment are involved in the purchase of services with the exception of shipping and receiving; in the purchase of an intangible service, this function is not required. Replacing the shipping-and-receiving function was maintenance/services. This function with the firm was often the overseer of the performance of the service.

In the purchase of services, only the purchasing and manufacturing functions were involved in the majority of cases. The participation of engineering was only about half of its participation in capital-equipment purchases. Top management participated in roughly half of the buying centers for services. The board of directors presence was almost nonexistent. Accounting and finance and sales and marketing roles were reduced. Miscellaneous others were still involved in almost half of the purchase situations.

The communication dyads that formed were subtly different from the pattern found in the capital-equipment-purchase process. While the four functions of purchasing, engineering, manufacturing, and top management remained the most involved in the buying-decision process, the communication patterns changed to reflect some differences in the way purchases in this product class were conducted. While purchasing and engineering became the interface with the vendors as in capital-equipment purchases, the vendors contacted others in the firm to an increased extent. Engineering became the prime communicator, along with purchasing, to the maintenance/services function. Top management became more active in contacting others within the firm. Figure 5.7 depicts the typical buying center for the purchase of industrial services. Others involved within the firm occasionally included construction, architects, inspection office, laboratory, traffic manager, union representatives, legal office, personnel,

FIGURE 5. 7

The Probable Buying Center for Industrial-Service Purchases

The Probable Buying Center for Industrial Service Purchases

Organizational Boundary

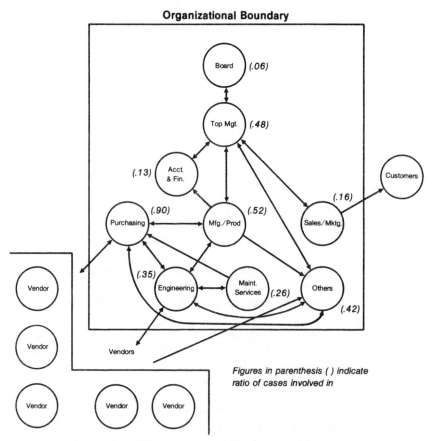

Figures in parenthesis ( ) indicate
ratio of cases involved in

requisition control, and the projects department. Others outside the firm involved customers, advertising agencies, testing laboratories, and managers at other companies in the same function. Again, this word of mouth was relatively limited except for that between a firm and its customers.

Manufacturing and production's communication with finance increased in proportion to their communication based upon their participation in capital-equipment purchases. The presence of miscellaneous others in the purchase of industrial services is one of the keys to understanding the buying center of industrial services. The vendors call on the "others" and get them to initiate the request for the contract of the services. There are strong communication links between these miscellaneous "others" and purchasing and top management.

It now seems appropriate, after having depicted the most probable buying centers for both capital equipment and industrial services, to examine the actual process of the buying behavior for these two classes of purchases. This is done in the next section, which discusses the flow of the buying process from first-recognized need to purchase and evaluation of the product or service.

THE INDUSTRIAL BUYING PROCESS

The BUYGRID model of Robinson, Faris, and Wind (1967) outlines eight buy phases that occur in the industrial-buying process. A closer examination of what actually occurs in the process of industrial-buying behavior indicates that, while the actions of the individuals in the buying center might be roughly categorized under these eight phases, the process is much more complex and much less straightforward than the BUYGRID model depicts.

First, the process is not always the smooth flow from start to finish that is depicted by the BUYGRID. In addition, some purchases include negotiation at several steps in the process. There is also as much action within the firm between buying-center participants as there is between the buying and selling firms. It is very difficult to generalize about the path that a buying process is likely to take because there are various different ways in which each major decision may be arrived at. A description of the various possible routes of the industrial-buying process is necessary for both purchase classes to highlight the complexity of this process.

The Flow of the Industrial Buying Process
for Capital Equipment

The recognition of a need or an opportunity is the point at which the discussion of industrial buying behavior usually begins. But the most important question is, How is this need or opportunity identified by the firm? That is, Just what really starts the buying process in motion? The two most common stimuli of industrial purchases of capital equipment are normal replacement of worn-out machinery or expansion of the production capability of a firm.

There are many other reasons, however, for the recognition of the need to perhaps purchase capital equipment. Outside vendor contact and the demonstration of products that can perform the same tasks faster, cheaper, or with less labor than currently owned equipment often start the buying process. Customer requests for a product or service that the company is currently not capable of providing also initiate the buying process. Marketing's decision to introduce a new product sometimes requires new equipment. Accidents that occur in the plant are often initiators of the search to find a better, safer way to produce the product, which leads to the consideration of different capital equipment. An environmental or legal requirement sometimes initiates the process. Emergency replacement and directed expansion by the board of directors are also factors that, while unexpected, lead to the recognition of the need to buy capital equipment. Finally, some purchases are accomplished simply out of habit, regardless of the need. This is similar to the expenditures of funds that have been budgeted simply because they have been budgeted, and, if they are not spent, it will be difficult to explain why not and to justify future budgets.

After this recognition of a need or opportunity, in many cases there is an immediate problem of just what to do. Discussions of solutions are conducted by members within the firm. Often approval is sought from higher levels of management to conduct feasibility studies on possible solutions. Preliminary contact with vendors is sometimes initiated to determine just what types of equipment are available, price ranges, and delivery times. Further research into the problem is often conducted. Sometimes the problem is just ignored with the hope that it will solve itself. But in general, this is a data-gathering stage in the buying process. Contact with friends in other companies is sometimes initiated to determine if others have ever encountered a similar problem, and, if so, how it has been solved. Trade shows are visited, catalogs are checked, and sometimes product testing is accomplished. As this stage converges toward the recognition of a general solution, discussions with top management, union officials, and other important functions within the firm are often conducted to ensure that the general solution meet with no major objections. This stage of the process usually ends with the development of preliminary estimates of requirements and sometimes with an attempt to justify the purchase by looking at return-on-investment (ROI) calculations.

If the purchase is not a normally planned purchase or one that needs budget approval, the next stage is a budget request. Normally, this is accomplished for all purchases of capital equipment except those that require only minor expenditures or are to be covered by a contract with a customer. Budget approval sometimes takes up to six months and is often accompanied by a series of internal negotiations between several parties with vested interests. Clearly, large allocations of funds in one direction limit the amount that can be allocated to other operations. Once budget approval is secured, the process generally moves into the more uniform stages of the buying process.

After budget approval, the next step in the process is usually the sending of a request for quotes to purchasing, although these two steps sometimes change place in the sequence; that is, sometimes the request for quotes is first placed with purchasing and then the budget-requesting procedure takes place. In yet other cases, purchasing never enters the picture, with all the transactions being conducted between manufacturing and the vendor, with purchasing being informed at the end of the process and required only to file the paperwork or to monitor for delivery. For the more technical purchases of equipment where there is not a standard model, specifications have to be developed. This is usually the responsibility of engineering working in conjunction with manufacturing. Sometimes safety or industrial engineering provide input to the development of specifications.

Concurrent with the design of the specifications is the development of the list of vendors to whom the specifications and an invitation to bid will be sent. Sometimes only one bidder is contacted. At other times the process is not accomplished through bidding but rather through negotiation. Sometimes the request of bids is used to identify the lowest bidders with whom subsequent negotiations are conducted. The development of the bidding list is one of the most interesting steps in the industrial buying, decision-making process. One company builds a bidders list by looking at satisfactory past purchases, talking to purchasing agents in other companies, and by referring to the yellow pages in the telephone book and the Thomas Register. Another company maintains a list of approved bidders at all times and getting on the list is totally unconnected with trying to make a current sale to the company. Once the preliminary list of bidders is compiled, it often has to be sent to the corporate purchasing department for approval. Sometimes engineering, manufacturing, and top management must approve the list. The list may also be open to addition and/or deletion of names by the various departments and functions. At other times, this is strictly the jurisdiction of purchasing. (To get on the approved-bidders list in one company, an inspection visit by representatives of purchasing, engineering, and quality assurance was required.) Remaining on the approved-bidders list is also sometimes a problem. Missing scheduled delivery dates, delivery of a product that fails to perform satisfactorily, or not providing prompt service or repair can quickly remove a bidder from the list. Once the list is finalized, requests for bids, along with the design specifications, are sent out. An equally interesting problem but one beyond the scope of this study is how vendors decided whether to bid or not.

Once bids go out, the company prepares to evaluate the bids when they begin to come back. Things that are checked for in the returned bids include delivery date, technical aspects of the design (whether they meet specifications), prices, quality, and reputation of the bidding company. In analyzing the bids, many companies prepare what is referred to as a tab sheet. This allows comparison of the bids on whatever dimensions the buying company has determined to be important. In the review of the bids, some companies check the quotes to justify the projected costs, calculate cost/benefit ratios, and weigh other intangibles in the decision. Other companies simply choose the lowest bidder. The decision is not always based on the lowest quoted price, however. Sometimes the bidding process is used as a preliminary stage to help develop a negotiation plan for the buying company. In this research it seemed that the larger companies were more interested in conducting negotiations as part of the buying process.

After deciding which bidder or product to buy, the process reaches the halfway point. Several very important discussions may take place before the actual contract is drawn up and signed. Yet to be determined are the method and terms of payment, any bond issues the buyer may require, exact delivery and installation requirements, and any service or warranty requirements of the buyer. The buyer and seller may take several months to work out the exact details of the purchase. The final price may have little or no relationship to the one that was quoted in the bidding process.

Sometimes this is the point at which the buying company begins to request approval for an appropriations request. Finally, the contract is drawn up and the order is placed. This is not the end of the buying process, however. Several aspects of the follow-up and product inspection are still required. If the equipment is to be built especially for the buyer, several periodic inspections may be conducted as the production takes place. Payment may not be made until the product successfully passes all stages of inspection. Sometimes payment is made in periodic payments. After the equipment is in place and in use, evaluation of its usefulness is made informally throughout the life of the product.

To believe that the industrial buying process is either uniform for most companies or that there is a set number·of steps through which the process smoothly flows is to not fully capture the complexity of the decision-making process. One company in the survey started out to buy a used vertical boring mill. They contacted ten vendors before they realized that their need could not best be met in this way. The company personnel then backtracked to the point of contacting vendors who built this type of equipment and continued the process from that point. In another company that failed to request that the bids be specified in total dollars, they received quotes priced per square foot. All of the vendors were requested to resubmit their bids. As

a third example of the complexity and lack of smooth, sequenced
stages, consider the company that contracts to have certain equipment built and delivered and makes periodic payments toward that
end only to have the vendor go bankrupt before final delivery.

Because of the complexity of these stages in the buying process,
it is also impossible to point to one function as having the sole responsibility for that step in the buying process. Previous research
has indicated that the purchasing department is responsible for preparing the bidders' list and engineering draws up the specifications.
This is too much a simplification of the process, as this discussion
should point out.

The Flow of the Industrial Buying
Process for Services

In the buying process for services, there are several distinct
differences from, but also quite a few similarities to, the process
found in the purchase of capital equipment.

The buying process for an industrial service also begins with
the recognition of a need or opportunity, but what generates this is
sometimes different from the stimuli that initiate the capital-equipment-purchase process.

Because many services are contracted on a yearly basis, the requirement exists, then, to review once a year the performance of that
service and make the determination of whether to continue it and, if so,
with the same vendor or not. But not all services are needed on a con-
tinual basis. Some are required only periodically and others only once.
Some of the specific stimuli for the initiation of the purchase of an industrial service include the need for a site survey because of a contemplated expansion (a one-time requirement), the need to relieve a
backlog in the drafting department without hiring another draftsman (a
periodic requirement), special customer orders, and the installation
of a fire-prevention system.

This research showed that when the need for a certain task to be
performed is recognized, often the first step is to review the internal
skills that exist within a company to determine if the service can be
performed by current employees. On the other hand, sometimes the
service is currently being performed by company employees but unsat-
isfactorily from one or more perspectives. If it is determined that the
skills do not exist to perform the service internally or that other good
reasons exist to have the service contracted, the next step in the process is often that of internal coordination with the appropriate parties.
(In the purchase of one very special service, an entire team was
formed with company employees to investigate the various effects this

service would have on the departments and divisions within the company and to develop plans to ease any problem areas within the firm.) The examination of available alternatives is accomplished and preliminary vendor inquiries are often performed. A requisition is sometimes developed to formalize the general procedure and a specific description of exactly what the service should accomplish is written. At other times, however, the exact details of the service are never specified but only assumed. In some cases, general goals are developed to be discussed with each of the interested vendors. If the details of the service are specified, they are reviewed internally by any one of a number of different functions. Sometimes additional details are added. In a few cases, the legal function reviews the desired service specifications for any possible legal ramifications such as liability.

Next a bid list is developed. An overriding concern in the development of the bid list for the purchase of a service seemed to be the reputation of the vendor. This seems to be because of the intangible nature of a service. Many of the cases in this research concerned with the purchase of services involved only one vendor. If a vendor had successfully performed the service before or was currently performing the service in a satisfactory manner, that vendor was the only one solicited. This was not always the case, however; in at least one company the policy existed of always getting bids from more than one vendor with the strategy of passing the contract around between the two lowest bidders. Once the bid list is developed, it may be subjected to corporate approval.

In several cases, before the bid requests were sent out, all potential bidders were called together at the potential buyer's facility for either private talks or general sessions to clarify and answer questions. Details of the exact need were discussed with the vendors. It seemed that it was a necessary step because of the problem of writing tight specifications on an intangible service.

Once the bid list has been developed and any necessary meetings have been conducted, the requests for proposals are sent out. In some cases that did not use the bidding system, negotiations were conducted with one or more vendors.

Selection of the vendor was based on a number of criteria, not always the lowest price. In some cases, the proposal was accepted if it was within the budget and technically sound. Previous experience and reputation played an important part in the decision. Once the desired vendor was identified, the request often required internal approval. Sometimes negotiations were conducted.

Notification was accomplished by letter, by phone, or in person. Details of the contract were worked out. If the contract was new, it was usually examined by legal counsel. The method of payment was established along with a completion schedule. As the service was performed, inspections were conducted in some cases. In other in-

FIGURE 5.8

Participation in Capital-Equipment Purchases

Steps in the Buying Process for Industrial Services	Purchasing	Engineering	Mfg/Prod.	Acct/Fin.	Sales/Mkt.	Top Mgt.	Board/Owner	Receiving/Shipping	Others	Vendors	Average Number Involved
1 Initiation Need Recognition Fact Finding General Solution	7	14	20	4	3	12	2	0	8	2	2.5
2 Specification Specific Solution Preparing Written Specification	7	15	21	1	1	6	1	0	3	6	2.0
2a Approval of Purchase	2	1	11	5	2	14	6	0	4	0	1.5

3 Search
Supplier Search
Acquisition of
  Proposals
Evaluation of
  Proposals
	22	11	12	5	2	10	2	0	5	0	2.2

3a Selection of Supplier	8	9	17	4	2	13	2	0	9	0	2.0
4 Formalization Negotiation Contact Payment	24	6	7	8	0	10	1	6	7	31	2.2
5 Evaluation Performance Satisfaction	18	11	18	0	2	6	0	6	14	0	2.4
TOTAL CASES OF INVOLVEMENT (31)	30	20	23	8	10	20	6	8	17	31	

stances, a final inspection or evaluation was conducted. In a few cases, no inspection or evaluation was conducted.

From the discussions of the purchase processes for capital equipment and industrial services, it should be realized that there are some procedures that appear with regularity, sometimes even in the same sequence. It is helpful to try to identify these steps in the process and determine who exerts what type of influence in them, but it should also be remembered that this is a simplification of some very complex processes. To date most research has attempted to

FIGURE 5.9

Participation in Industrial-Service Purchases

Steps in the Buying Process for Industrial Services	Purchasing	Engineering	Mfg/Prod.	Acct/Fin.	Sales/Mkt.	Top Mgt.	Board/Owner	Maint. Ser.	Others	Vendors	Average Number Involved
1 Initiation Need Recognition Fact Finding General Solution	14	9	12	0	2	10	1	6	8	12	2.0
2 Specification Specific Solution Preparing Written Specification	17	6	12	3	1	9	0	6	5	14	2.0
2a Approval of Purchase	8	8	10	4	2	13	2	4	5	0	1.8

3 Search
Supplier Search
Acquisition of
  Proposals
Evaluation of
  Proposals
	22	7	13	3	2	6	9	5	6	0	2.0

3a Selection of Supplier	14	6	12	1	2	10	1	7	9	0	2.0
4 Formalization Negotiation Contact Payment	23	6	8	4	1	5	0	3	8	31	1.9
5 Evaluation Performance Satisfaction	14	9	14	0	1	8	0	7	9	0	2.0
TOTAL CASES OF INVOLVEMENT (31)	28	11	16	4	5	15	2	8	13	31	

identify the one function within a firm that was responsible for a particular step in the process. The results of this research have often been conflicting. This has occurred for several, now rather obvious, reasons. First, the nature of "responsibility" was never thoroughly clarified, and as this research has discovered, a number of different functions may be involved at any particular stage in the buying process and usually are. Figures 5.8 and 5.9 depict the involvement of the different functional areas within a firm and important others in the stages of industrial buying behavior.

6

THE SOCIAL NATURE OF INDUSTRIAL BUYING BEHAVIOR: RETROSPECT AND PROSPECT

This chapter presents the major conclusions to be drawn from this study. The implications and limitations of this research are also examined. Finally, directions for future research are suggested based upon the results of this research.

The primary aim of this study was to develop and test an improved conceptualization of industrial buying behavior, one that drew concepts and used methodologies from organizational-behavior and social-science areas. It is believed that industrial buying behavior is a social phenomenon and needs to be studied at a social, rather than individual, level. In order to accomplish this, the buying center and the communication network that evolved from the process of industrial-buying behavior was examined in 31 companies that had made purchases of capital equipment and industrial services.

While previous approaches to industrial-buying behavior have generally provided conflicting results and little understanding of the complex phenomenon, the research in this study indicates that if an interactional and transactional viewpoint is applied, the purchasing process becomes clearer.

The study defined and operationalized five dimensions of the buying center—that group of individuals who become involved in the purchasing process for a particular product or service.

Lateral involvement: The extent to which various departments, divisions, or functional specialists become involved in the purchasing-communication network;

Vertical involvement: The extent to which various levels of the organizational hierarchy get involved in the purchasing-communication network;

Extension: The total number of individuals involved in the communication network;

Connectedness: The extent to which individuals involved in the purchasing process are in communication with others involved; and

Centrality of purchasing: The degree to which purchasing personnel are central to the buying-center communication network.

A number of independent variables that measured structural aspects of the buying firm, purchase-situation attributes, and characteristics of the purchasing managers involved were examined to determine how they affected the dimensions of the buying center. The structural variables of the firm measured the organization's size, formalization, centralization, and complexity. The purchase-situation variables measured the importance, novelty, and complexity of the equipment or service that was purchased. The characteristics of the purchasing manager could be divided into three factors: experience, specialization, and achievement. It was found that the buying center's structure is affected by variables from each of the groups of independent variables. That is, the structural properties of a firm, the attributes of a particular purchase situation, and the characteristics of the purchasing manager involved all affect the composition of the buying center for that particular purchase.

Although the previous chapter presented the results of the qualitative and quantitative analyses, this chapter will review those results with the intention of highlighting the major conclusions that can be drawn from them.

SUMMARY OF THE RESULTS AND
CONCLUSIONS TO BE DRAWN

The results were reported in five sections in Chapter 5. Simple statistics and descriptive correlations in the data were reported first. The second section reported the results from factor analysis of the three sets of independent variables. Regression analysis was used to examine the effect of the independent variables on the dimensions of the buying center and the purchasing manager's centrality in the buying-center's communication network as calculated using sociometric techniques. These regression analyses for both equipment and service purchases were reported in the third section on results. The fourth section examined the aggregate communication networks of each purchase class. In these aggregate communication networks, participation is depicted by the main diagonal, while cells off the main diagonal depict dyad formation between the various functional departments (who communicates with whom). In the final section dealing with the results of this research, a qualitative description of the flow of tasks involved in the industrial buying process was presented. A task-involvement matrix showing which functional areas were involved with each task for both services and equipment was developed.

Simple Statistics and Interesting Correlations

The size of companies involved in the study ranged from $5 million in sales to $8.6 billion. The smallest company employed only 59 employees, while the largest employed over 160,000.

The complexity of companies varied from those that had only one division and a single operating location to one that had 39 divisions and subsidiaries and over 200 separate operating locations.

Most of the companies that participated in the study were industrial manufacturers. The degree of formalization of these companies varied greatly. Some had no limits on the amount various ranks in the company were authorized to commit and no purchasing policies manual. Others had well-structured limits on spending and elaborate corporate procedures dealing with purchasing. The amount of written communication concerning a particular purchase increased with the perceived importance of that purchase. However, the amount of written communication as a percentage of all communication (both written and spoken) decreased as the perceived importance of the purchase increased.

Conclusion 1: Communication in the buying center increases as the purchase becomes more important. Spoken communication increases at a greater rate than written communication. Thus, word of mouth is an important force in the industrial-buying process.

The purchasing departments were located at various levels within the 31 firms and the centralization of the purchasing function varied from highly centralized with all purchasing being done at the corporate level to highly decentralized with each separate operating location making all of its own purchases.

The purchase situations examined consisted of recent purchases of capital equipment and industrial services. On average, each purchase was considered important. Purchases of capital equipment were viewed as more important than purchases of services. The purchases of services had a greater variance on the perceived-importance dimension than capital equipment. The number of vendors involved in the buying process was positively correlated with the perceived importance of a service purchase. Primary purchases or those directly involved in a company's business functions were perceived as more important. The more important a purchase was perceived to be, the more likely it would be negotiated between buyer and seller.

Conclusion 2: The perceived importance of a purchase plays an important role in determining the form of buyer-seller interaction.

The perceived complexity of the purchase situations varied greatly. The novelty of a purchase situation had an interesting interaction effect with the purchase class. The more novel a purchase situation was for capital equipment, the more likely the purchase was to be negotiated. The more novel a service-purchase situation, the more likely it was to be settled through competitive bidding.

Conclusion 3: The novelty of a purchase situation has an effect on the form of buyer-seller interaction. The effect is moderated, however, by the product class of the purchase.

Stepwise-Linear-Regression Analysis

The regression analysis proved relatively successful. The four dimensions of the buying center were found to be affected by structural variables of the firms and purchase-situation attributes. Characteristics of the purchasing manager had little effect on the dimensions of the buying center. On the other hand, the structural variables of the firm and the purchase-situation attributes explained little variance in the centrality of the purchasing manager in the communication network of the buying center. The characteristics of the purchasing manager did explain a fair amount of the variance in centrality for purchases of industrial services. Most of the regressions explained from 40 percent to 50 percent of the variance in the dependent variables. For purchases of capital equipment, the variables that had the greatest effect on buying-center dimensions were the perceived importance of the purchase, the limits a company set on authorization of funds, the perceived formalization of a company's buying policies, the degree of centralization of the purchasing function, the size of the company, and how often the purchase was made. The integrative complexity of the buying-center communication network was affected by the percentage of communication that was written, whether a manual of purchasing policies existed, the number of individuals involved both within the buying center and as vendors, and the size of the company. The centrality of the purchasing manager in the communication network was affected only by the number of vendors involved.

For purchases of industrial services, the variables that had the greatest effect on buying-center dimensions were the time it took to complete a purchase, the centralization of the purchasing function, the formalization of the purchasing process, the complexity of the buying firm, the size of the buying firm, and the number of vendors involved. The centrality of the purchasing manager is highly dependent upon whether or not he is certified as a purchasing manager.

Conclusion 4: The dimensions of the buying center operationalized in this research are affected by structural variables of the firm and purchase-situation attributes. The centrality of the purchasing manager in the communication network is more a function of the individual differences of the purchasing managers than other independent variables examined here.

Aggregate Communication Networks

By collapsing the communication networks of the individual cases examined in each purchase class, an aggregate communication network can be constructed for each purchase class. The main diagonal of these matrixes depicts participation by function while the off-diagonal cells depict communication between various functions. For purchases of capital equipment, the buying center consists most often of the purchasing, engineering, production, and top management functions. For services, purchasing, production, and top management most often make up the buying center.

Interesting patterns of communication can also be detected. For instance, purchasing and engineering tend to interface with the vendors, while production communicates with top management.

Conclusion 5: By approaching industrial buying behavior from a social perspective, interesting patterns of interaction can be detected in the buying center that could provide important information for marketing strategies.

The Qualitative Description of the Flow of Tasks in Industrial-Buying Behavior

To describe industrial buying behavior as a chronological process with predetermined stages of decision processes taking place distorts what actually happens. While certain tasks occur with regularity, they do not always follow the same order, and often the process is iterative with certain tasks being repeated more than once. In the case of capital-equipment purchases, most tasks involve two or more functional areas, while for services two or less functions are involved.

Conclusion 6: Finding the key buying influence in a purchase decision may be a highly complex, if not impossible, process. It may be much more useful to examine who influences which tasks and act accordingly.

IMPLICATIONS

Emphasis in the past on individualistic and stimulus-response approaches to industrial buying behavior appears to have offered only partial accounts of purchasing processes. More important, these approaches have led to the mistaken belief that industrial buying is something that a purchasing manager does rather than (as this study has shown) a socially negotiated outcome of a transaction in which many individuals within the buying organization and in the selling organization are engaged. By applying a transactional or dyadic approach, all of those interactions are captured in a model that begins to move toward a systems perspective of industrial buying behavior.

Industrial organizations have many functional specialists who may be involved in various ways in purchase decisions. In looking for a single decider in the industrial buying process, the fact that a company is really often compartmentalized by task is lost. In the 62 cases studied, there was not one in which only a single individual within a firm made all the decisions solely on his own. Different functions play different roles in the stages of the buying process. It is impossible to determine who had the greatest influence on a purchase decision. Consider a situation in which top management alone will pick the supplier of a particular product or service. If engineering and purchasing develop the bidding list and write the specifications, who really exerted the greatest influence?

Industrial buying-behavior research must move beyond searches for the real buying influence. This study provides several improved ways in which to examine participation and influence in the buying center that evolves for a particular purchase. Research must begin to examine the entire process of industrial buying behavior and attempt to understand who has what influence under which conditions. This study provides a first step in two key purchase classes.

In addition, the research presented here indicates that both those who feel the purchasing manager has a great deal of influence in the industrial buying process and those who do not are incorrectly conceptualizing the problem. Instead of seeking to determine whether or not the purchasing manager has influence over the buying-decision process, researchers ought to be asking, When does the purchasing manager have influence in the buying decision? By using sociometric techniques, it was possible to indicate that the purchasing manager's centrality in the buying center is not fixed. This centrality in the communication network can be calculated for each buying-center participant. Research in small-group dynamics and other areas of organizational behavior has shown that centrality is often correlated with status and influence. Thus, centrality in the communication network may represent an objective measure of influence on the purchasing process.

LIMITATIONS OF THE RESEARCH

While a number of significant relationships were identified in this research, the major limitations of this study lie in the size and generalizability of the sample. Although over 240 interviews were conducted, only two purchases in 31 firms were examined. Some of the statistical procedures would be more appropriate for larger size samples. The degree of generalizability is also questionable. All of the companies in the sample were Pittsburgh based. The sample contains an overrepresentation of steel manufacturers. In addition, Pittsburgh-based companies may be different from companies located in other parts of the United States.

Only two purchase classes were examined (capital equipment and industrial services). Industrial buying decisions also involve purchases of raw materials, component parts, and supplies. The buying centers for these purchases may be entirely different from those of capital equipment and services.

The factor analysis of the variables that measured the purchase-situation attributes provided little empirical support for the hypothesized concepts. An industrial-purchase-situation typology would prove useful in many ways.

DIRECTIONS FOR FUTURE RESEARCH

Based upon the successful outcome of this research, several directions for future research can be suggested. The methodology is sound and has produced the first study in which structural dimensions of the buying organizations have significantly correlated with buying-center composition.

The first direction for future research should be toward increasing the data base in several directions. Adding more companies would make the data base more generalizable and more amenable to regression and factor analysis. At least 100 companies should be included in the sample. In addition, different purchase classes should be added to the data base. We know what the buying centers for capital equipment and services look like and how they vary, but the buying centers for raw materials, component parts, and supplies may be entirely different. These buying centers should be constructed using the snowball sampling techniques described in this study. The ideal data base would consist of at least 100 randomly selected firms in which the purchase of one product was examined from each purchase class (raw materials, component parts, supplies, capital equipment, and services).

Other directions for research suggested by this study include a more in-depth examination of the variance in centrality of all buying-center participants. This research examined the centrality of the purchasing manager in each buying center. By understanding the participation of each function in the buying center, a greater understanding of industrial buying behavior will be obtained.

The most important questions that must be addressed in future research on industrial buying behavior still remain. Who participates in which tasks in the organizational-purchasing process? What is the degree of influence of each purchasing-process participant? Under what conditions do various participants exert their influence?

This research has provided the methodology to examine these questions and has made a start on the necessary work in two purchase classes. A great deal of work remains to be done. The directions for future research have been indicated.

APPENDIX 1

INTERVIEW SCHEDULE

Purchasing Manager--Questions

First some questions about yourself

- What is your position in your company?

- How long have you worked for your company? In purchasing?

- How many years purchasing experience do you have in total?

- Your level of education?

- Are you a Certified Purchasing Manager?

- What level in the company is your purchasing department?

> Corporate
>
> Divisional
>
> Plant

Now I would like to ask you some questions about purchasing management in your company

- How is the purchasing function organized within your company?

> Centralized
>
> Decentralized
>
> Some bought at corporate level/some at divisional/plant level (if so get some specifics) i.e.,
> > What corporate_____
> > What divisional_____
> > What plant_____

- How many people work in your purchasing department?

- Is there a manual of purchasing policies in your company?

- What (if any) are the $(dollar) limits the various ranks in purchasing are authorized to commit?

- On a scale of 1 to 10 how formalized would you say your company's purchasing policies/procedures are in comparison to other companies.

> 1 2 3 4 5 6 7 8 9 10
>
> Not at all   Extremely
> formalized   Formalized

Now, some questions about your company in general

- What is the main business of your company?

- How many divisions are there?

153

. How many separate plants/operating locations are there?

At this point I would like you to identify/think of a specific purchase of capital equipment made recently by your company in which you were involved

. What was the equipment/machinery that was purchased?

. For what level of the company was this purchased? Corporate/ Divisional/Plant(s) How many?

. What was the equipment to be used for?

. Who else besides yourself was involved in the purchase of this equipment?

. Of these people who did you have direct communications with?

. What percentage of this communication was written; what percentage spoken?

Name	Position	Direct Communication (If Yes,%)
		Yes_____ No_____
		Written_____
		Spoken_____

.What was the procedure involved in making this purchase? Starting with who first identified the need or opportunity

> For this equipment?
> Then what happened?
> Then what happened?
> Then what happened?

Finishing with who inspected or evaluated the equipment once in place?

. On a scale of 1 to 10 how important was this purchase compared with all the other purchases your company makes?

$$1 \quad 2 \quad 3 \quad 4 \quad 5 \quad 6 \quad 7 \quad 8 \quad 9 \quad 10$$

Not at all   Of the utmost
important   importance

. How many vendors/suppliers were contacted in regard to this procedure?

154

. On a scale of from 1 to 10 how complex or difficult to evaluate were the alternatives available for this purchase?

```
1  2  3  4  5  6  7  8  9  10
```

Extremely   Extremely
simple and   complex and
easy to   difficult to
evaluate   evaluate

. How often does your company make purchases of this type of equipment?

. When was the last time your company made a purchase similar to this one?

At this point I would like you to identify/think of a specific purchase of an industrial service made recently by your company in which you were involved

. What was the service that was purchased?

. For what level of the company was this purchased? Corporate/Divisional/Plant(s)--How many?

. Who else beside yourself was involved in the purchase of this service?

. Of these people, who did you have direct communications with? What percentage of this communication was written? What percentage spoken?

Name   Position   Direct Communication (If yes,%)
_____   _____   _____ Yes _____ No
                                  Written_____Spoken_____

. What was the procedure involved in making this purchase?

Starting with who first identified the need or opportunity for this service?

                        Then what happened?
                        Then what happened?
                        Then what happened?

Finishing with who evaluated the performance of the service?

. On a scale of 1 to 10 how important was this purchase compared with the other purchases your company makes?

```
1  2  3  4  5  6  7  8  9  10
```

Not at all   Of the utmost
important   importance

. How many vendors/contractors were contacted in regard to the performance of this service?

. How long did the entire process take from first recognized need to the final purchase conclusion?

. On a scale of 1 to 10 <u>how complex or difficult to evaluate were</u> the <u>alternatives</u> available for this purchase?

```
     1   2   3   4   5   6   7   8   9   10
   ┣━━━━━━━━━━━━━━━━━━━━━━━┿━━━━━━━━━━━━━━━━━━━━━━━┫
```

Extremely	Extremely
simple and	complex and
easy to	difficult to
evaluate	evaluate

. How often does your company purchase this type of service?

. When was the last time your company made a purchase similar to this?

It appears that _____ was (were) quite deeply involved in these purchases. Would it be possible for me to talk briefly with them? I have a few questions I would like to ask each of them.

Get telephone numbers or addresses (office number)

Questions for Others

Someone I have already interviewed said you might have been involved in the purchase of _____ by your company.

. Do you remember being involved in this purchase?

. What is your position in your company?

. What part did you play in the purchase of this equipment or service?

. Who else besides yourself was involved in this purchase? Any one outside of your company?

Of these people who did you have direct communications with? What percentage of this communication was written and what percentage spoken?

Name   Position   Direct Communication (If yes,%)

                                         Yes_____No_____
                                         Written_____Spoken_____

. On a scale of 1 to 10 how important was this purchase compared with all the other purchases your company makes?

                    1 2 3 4 5 6 7 8 9 10

                    Not at all   Of the utmost
                    important   importance

. On a scale of 1 to 10 how complex or difficult to evaluate were the alternatives available for this purchase?

                    1 2 3 4 5 6 7 8 9 10

                    Extremely   Extremely
                    simple and   complex and
                    easy to   difficult to
                    evaluate   evaluate

. On a scale of 1 to 10 how formalized would you say your company's purchasing policies/procedures are in comparison to other companies?

                    1 2 3 4 5 6 7 8 9 10

                    Not at all   Extremely
                    formalized   formalized

APPENDIX 2

STEPWISE REGRESSION ANALYSES

Capital Equipment

Stepwise Regression Analysis of Lateral Involvement

in the Buying Center System

Step	Variable	F Ratio	Regression Coefficient	Multiple R	Multiple R^2	Adjusted R^2
1	IMPORT	1.2	0.23	0.49	0.24	0.22
	EMP	4.6	0.42	0.55	0.30	0.25
3	DIVSUB	2.3	-0.32	0.59	0.35	0.28
4	OFTEN	2.1	-0.23	0.62	0.38	0.29
5	WRITEN	3.1	0.34	0.65	0.42	0.31
6	NEWNESS	1.4	0.25	0.67	0.45	0.31
7	PLANTS	1.2	-0.18	0.69	0.48	0.32

df 7,22

Regression F 2.91   Standard Error 1.30

$p < .05$

Capital Equipment

Stepwise Regression Analysis of Vertical Involvement in the Buying Center System

Step	Variable	F Ratio	B Regression Coefficient	Multiple R	Multiple R^2	Adjusted R^2
1	IMPORT	12.5	0.45	0.47	0.22	0.19
2	LIMIT$	12.6	-0.52	0.63	0.40	0.36
3	FORMAL	5.3	-0.31	0.69	0.48	0.42
4	DIVSUB	3.6	0.26	0.74	0.54	0.47
5	PURORG	6.1	0.36	0.76	0.58	0.49
6	OFTEN	3.8	-0.24	0.79	0.63	0.53
7	VENDORS	3.7	0.26	0.83	0.68	0.58

df 7,22   Standard Error 0.61

Regression F 6.73

p < .01

Capital Equipment

Stepwise Regression Analysis of the Buying Center System's Extension

Step	Variable	F Ratio	B Regression Coefficient	Multiple R	Multiple R^2	Adjusted R^2
1	IMPORT	9.5	0.48	0.58	0.33	0.31
2	LIMIT$	3.8	-0.28	0.68	0.46	0.41
3	OFTEN	4.5	-0.29	0.74	0.55	0.49
4	MANUAL	1.1	-0.17	0.75	0.57	0.50
5	SALES	3.8	0.32	0.77	0.59	0.50
6	PRIMARY	1.9	0.19	0.78	0.61	0.51
7	FORMAL	1.8	-0.22	0.79	0.63	0.51
8	PLANTS	1.6	-0.18	0.81	0.66	0.53

df 8,21

Regression F 5.03   Standard Error 3.45

$p < .01$

Capital Equipment

Stepwise Regression Analysis of the Buying Center's Connectedness

Step	Variable	F Ratio	B Regression Coefficient	Multiple R	Multiple R^2	Adjusted R^2
1	WRITEN	11.1	-0.52	0.45	0.20	0.18
2	MANUAL	13.0	-0.53	0.59	0.35	0.30
3	DIFF	9.3	-0.43	0.67	0.45	0.39
4	SALES	4.5	0.34	0.72	0.52	0.45
5	VENDORS	4.3	0.29	0.75	0.58	0.49
6	PURORG	2.7	0.23	0.79	0.62	0.52

df 6, 23

Regression F = 6.29   Standard Error 7.97

$p < .01$

Capital Equipment

Stepwise Regression Analysis of the Centrality of the

Purchasing Manager in the Buying Center System

Step	Variable	F Ratio	B Regression Coefficient	Multiple R	Multiple R^2	Adjusted R^2
1	VENDORS	4.4	0.37	0.31	0.10	0.07
2	PRIMARY	3.4	-0.32	0.45	0.20	0.14

df 2, 27   Standard Error = 0.19

Regression F = 3.35

$p < .05$

Capital Equipment

Stepwise Regression Analysis of Purchasing Manager Attributes
and Purchasing Department Characteristics on PM Centrality

Step	Variable	F Ratio	B Regression Coefficient	Multiple R	Multiple R^2	Adjusted R^2
1	NUMPPL	1.7	-0.23	0.25	0.06	0.03
2	CPM	2.0	0.26	0.33	0.10	0.05
3	WKCO	1.0	-0.18	0.38	0.14	0.05

df 3, 27

Regression F = 1.49   Standard Error = 0.22

$p < .10$

Industrial Services

Stepwise Regression Analysis of Vertical Involvement in the Buying Center System

Step	Variable	F Ratio	B Regression Coefficient	Multiple R	Multiple R^2	Adjusted R^2
1	TIME	10.0	0.33	0.56	0.32	0.29
2	IMPORT	2.3	0.26	0.68	0.46	0.42
3	PLANTS	3.7	0.30	0.73	0.53	0.47
4	PURORG	8.0	0.34	0.76	0.58	0.51
5	FORMAL	6.5	-0.34	0.79	0.63	0.55
6	SALES	3.9	0.31	0.82	0.67	0.58
7	LASTIME	3.4	0.24	0.84	0.71	0.62

df 7, 22

Regression F = 7.71   Standard Error = 0.60

$p < .01$

Industrial Services

Stepwise Regression Analysis of Lateral Involvement in the Buying Center System

Step	Variable	F Ratio	B Regression Coefficient	Multiple R	Multiple R^2	Adjusted R^2
1	NEWNESS	1.7	0.23	0.50	0.25	0.22
2	TIME	8.5	0.47	0.59	0.34	0.30
3	DIVSUB	8.5	0.44	0.64	0.41	0.34
4	FORMAL	2.0	-0.22	0.68	0.47	0.38
5	WRITEN	5.7	0.38	0.71	0.50	0.40
6	LASTIME	4.4	0.34	0.74	0.55	0.43
7	PRIMARY	4.8	-0.49	0.76	0.57	0.43
8	IMPORT	3.7	0.42	0.78	0.62	0.47
9	MANUAL	1.6	-0.22	0.80	0.64	0.48

df 9, 20

Regression F = 4.00   Standard Error = 0.86

$p < .01$

Industrial Services

Stepwise Regression Analysis of the Buying Center's Extension

Step	Variable	F Ratio	B Regression Coefficient	Multiple R	Multiple R^2	Adjusted R^2
1	TIME	24.1	0.50	0.61	0.37	0.35
2	IMPORT	4.1	0.22	0.71	0.50	0.46
3	EMP	17.0	0.46	0.76	0.57	0.52
4	FORMAL	15.0	-0.44	0.82	0.67	0.62
5	VENDORS	9.6	0.32	0.87	0.76	0.71
6	LASTIME	2.5	0.16	0.88	0.78	0.73

df 6,23

Regression F = 13.8   Standard Error = 1.6

$p < .01$

Industrial Services

Stepwise Regression Analysis of the Buying Center's Connectedness

Step	Variable	F Ratio	B Regression Coefficient	Multiple R	Multiple R^2	Adjusted R^2
1	DIFF	23.0	-0.69	0.55	0.31	0.28
2	WRITEN	3.8	-0.27	0.65	0.43	0.38
3	VENDORS	5.0	0.36	0.73	0.54	0.49
4	PRIMARY	3.0	0.23	0.76	0.57	0.50
5	OFTEN	4.4	-0.30	0.78	0.61	0.53
6	MANUAL	1.9	-0.19	0.81	0.65	0.56
7	PURORG	1.6	0.17	0.82	0.68	0.57

df 7, 22

Regression F = 6.5   Standard Error = 10.9

$p < .01$

Industrial Services

Stepwise Regression Analysis of the Centrality of the Purchasing Manager

in the Buying Center System

Step	Variable	F Ratio	B Regression Coefficient	Multiple R	Multiple R^2	Adjusted R^2
1	LIMIT$	8.2	0.53	0.34	0.12	0.09
2	TIME	2.8	-0.33	0.43	0.18	0.12
3	IMPORT	3.8	-0.51	0.46	0.21	0.12
4	COMPLEX	2.1	0.33	0.53	0.29	0.17
5	PRIMARY	1.0	0.25	0.56	0.32	0.17

df 5, 24

Regression F = 2.21   Standard Error = 0.27

p < .10

Industrial Services

Stepwise Regression Analysis of Purchasing Manager Centrality in the Buying Center System
as a Function of the Purchasing Manager & Department

Step	Variable	F Ratio	B Coefficient	Multiple R	Multiple R^2	Adjusted R^2
1	CPM	13.6	0.52	0.57	0.32	0.30
2	PMPOS	1.3	-0.17	0.62	0.39	0.35
3	TOTYRSP	6.9	0.48	0.68	0.46	0.40
4	DPTLEV	3.5	-0.29	0.70	0.50	0.42
5	WKCO	2.7	-0.30	0.74	0.55	0.46

df 5, 25   Standard Error = 0.22

Regression F = 6.01

$p < .01$

APPENDIX 3

PARTIAL CORRELATIONS BETWEEN CRITERION AND PREDICTOR VARIABLES

PARTIAL CORRELATIONS BETWEEN PREDICTION AND CRITERION
VARIABLES FOR CAPITAL EQUIPMENT PURCHASES

Criterion Variable & Hypothesized Relationship	Size SALES EMP	Complexity DIVSUB PLANTS	Organizational Formalization MANUAL LIMITS FORMAL WRITTEN	Centralization PURORG	Importance IMPORT PRIMARY	Purchase Novelty OFTEN LASTIME NEWNESS	Complexity COMPLEX VENDORS TIME
Vertical Involvement	– – –.12 –.14	– – +.31 –.05	– – – – –.28 –.61*** –.42** +.23	+ +.43*	+ + +.60*** +.18	– + + –.36* +.09 –.09	+.01 +.24 –.03
Lateral Involvement	+ + .27 +.34*	+ + –.29 –.17	? ? ? ? –.23 –.22 –.15 +.29	– –.96	+ + +.24 +.07	– + + –.22 +.07 +.22	+.03 –.01 –.12
Extension	+ + +.30 +.27	+ + –.11 –.17	? ? ? ? –.30 –.48** –.36* +.23	– +.07	+ + +.52** +.30	– + + –.39* +.06 +.05	.00 +.10 –.10
Connectedness	– – +.38* +.47**	– – –.37* +.18	? ? ? ? –.54** +.01 +.17 –.05	+ +.17	+ + –.21 –.36*	– + + +.26 +.04 +.45**	+.09 +.59*** +.05
Centrality of the Purchasing Manager	+ + +.21 +.18	+ + –.17 –.15	? ? ? ? –.06 –.06 –.10 +.16	? –.16	– – –.13 –.33	+ – – –.09 +.37* +.27	+.10 +.40* –.21

PARTIAL CORRELATIONS BETWEEN PREDICTION AND CRITERION
VARIABLES FOR INDUSTRIAL SERVICE PURCHASES

Concept and Predictor Variables

Criterion Variable & Hypothesized Relationship	Size: SALES	Size: EMP	Complexity: DIVSUB	Complexity: PLANTS	Formalization: MANUAL	Formalization: LIMITS	Formalization: FORMAL	Formalization: WRITEN	Centralization: PURORG	Importance: IMPORT	Importance: PRIMARY	Novelty: OFTEN	Novelty: LASTIME	Novelty: NEWNESS	Complexity: COMPLEX	Complexity: VENDORS	Complexity: TIME
Vertical Involvement	− +.26	− +.37*	− +.22	− +.57***	− −.17	− −.12	− −.45**	− +.21	+ +.61**	+ +.31	+ −.04	− −.13	+ +.48**	+ +.22	− +.15	− −.42**	− +.53**
Lateral Involvement	+ −.12	+ −.08	+ +.49**	+ +.04	? −.22	? +.16	? −.37*	? +.32*	− −.15	+ +.11	+ −.18	+ −.02	+ +.39*	+ +.26	+ +.07	+ −.22	+ +.57***
Extension	+ +.47**	+ +.58***	+ +.08	+ +.24	? −.22	? +.13	? −.57**	? +.33*	− +.14	+ +.33	+ .00	− +.03	+ +.43**	+ +.32	+ +.17	+ −.24	+ +.65***
Connectedness	− +.13	− +.26	− +.13	− −.11	? −.34*	? −.12	? −.21	? −.33*	+ +.32	+ +.31	+ +.29	− −.41**	+ +.10	+ −.27	+ +.14	+ +.31	+ +.10
Centrality of the Purchasing Manager	+ −.02	+ −.10	+ +.07	+ −.23	? −.14	? +.51**	? −.04	? +.17	? −.19	− −.24	− −.07	+ −.12	− −.04	− −.21	− +.20	− +.23	− −.19

APPENDIX 4

SUMMATIVE
COMMUNICATIONS NETWORKS

SUMMATIVE COMMUNICATION NETWORK MATRIX

CAPITAL EQUIPMENT PURCHASES

Cell Counts

Function	Pur-chasing	Engin-eering	Mfg./Prod.	Acctg./Finance	Sales/Mktg.	Top Mgt.	Board/Owner	Shipping/Rec.	Others	Vendors
Purchasing	.97	19 (10) + .61	14 (11) + .29	3 (4) - .10	4 (5) - .13	6 (10) - .19	1 (3) - .03	5 (4) + .16	10 (8) + .32	28 (15) + .90
Engineering	18 (10) + .58	.65	11 (7) + .35	2 (3) - .06	3 (3) ∅ .10	4 (7) - .13	1 (2) - .03	1 (3) - .03	7 (6) + .23	11 (10) ∅ .55
Mfg./Prod.	13 (11) + .2	12 (7) + .39	.74	3 (3) ∅ .10	5 (4) + .16	15 (7) + .48	0 (2) - .00	1 (3) - .03	8 (6) + .26	5 (11) - .16
Acctg./Finance	5 (4) + .16	1 (3) - .03	3 (3) ∅ .10	.26	1 (1) ∅ .03	4 (3) + .13	2 (1) + .06	1 (1) ∅ .03	0 (2) - .00	0 (4) - .00
Sales/Mktg.	3 (5) - .10	4 (3) - .13	6 (4) + .19	1 (1) ∅ .03	.32	4 (3) + .13	0 (1) - .00	0 (1) - .00	4 (3) + .13	2 (5) - .06
Top Mgt.	7 (10) - .23	3 (7) - .10	13 (7) + .42	5 (3) + .16	3 (3) ∅ .10	.65	3 (2) + .10	0 (3) - .00	1 (6) - .03	1 (10) - .03
Board/Owner	1 (3) - .03	2 (2) ∅ .06	2 (2) ∅ .06	2 (1) + .06	0 (1) - .00	2 (2) ∅ .06	.19	0 (1) - .00	0 (2) - .00	0 (3) - .00

Function	Pur-chasing	Engin-eering	Mfg./ Prod.	Acctg./ Finance	Sales/ Mktg.	Top Mgt.	Board/ Owner	Shipping/ Rec.	Others	Vendors
Shipping/Rec.	4 (4) Ø .13	3 (3) Ø .10	2 (3) - .06	1 (1) Ø .03	0 (1) - .00	1 (3) - .03	0 (1) - .00	.26	2 (2) Ø .06	2 (4) - .06
Others	8 (8) Ø .26	9 (6) + .26	10 (6) + .32	0 (2) - .00	4 (3) + .16	2 (6) - .16	0 (2) - .06	1 (2) - .03	.55	6 (10) - .19
Vendors	26 (15) + .81	11 (10) Ø .35	7 (11) - .23	0 (4) - .00	3 (5) - .10	1 (10) - .03	0 (3) - .00	4 (4) Ø .13	8 (9) Ø .26	1.0

TOTAL COMMUNICATION LINKS = 410

Main Diagonal Cells = % of involvement in 31 cases

Off Diagonal Cells =

Observed	(Expected)
more/less	
% of cases	

Others
  Inside--safety, IE, maintenance, personnel, projects, commercial
        department, etc.
  Outside--other purchasing managers, customers, other managers in
        other firms

180

SUMMATIVE COMMUNICATION NETWORK MATRIX
INDUSTRIAL SERVICE PURCHASES

Cell Counts

Function	Pur-chasing	Engin-eering	Mfg./Prod.	Acctg./Finance	Sales/Mktg.	Top Mgt.	Board/Owner	Maint. Services	Others	Vendors
Purchasing	.90	7 (5) + .23	9 (7) + .29	0 (2) - .00	1 (2) - .03	3 (7) - .10	0 (1) - .00	3 (4) - .10	9 (6) + .29	27 (14) + .87
Engineering	8 (5) + .29	.35	5 (3) + .16	1 (1) ∅ .03	0 (1) - .03	2 (3) - .06	0 (0) ∅ .00	2 (1) + .06	5 (2) + .16	6 (5) + .19
Mfg./Prod.	11 (7) + .35	4 (3) + .13	.52	2 (1) + .06	1 (1) ∅ .03	6 (4) + .19	0 (0) ∅ .00	2 (2) ∅ .06	5 (3) + .16	5 (8) - .16
Acctg./Finance	0 (2) - .00	0 (1) - .00	1 (1) ∅ .03	.13	0 (0) ∅	3 (1) + .10	0 (0) ∅ .00	0 (1) - .00	0 (1) - .00	1 (2) - .03
Sales/Mktg.	2 (2) ∅ .06	0 (1) - .00	1 (1) ∅ .03	0 (0) ∅ .00	.16	3 (1) + .10	0 (0) ∅ .00	1 (1) ∅ .03	2 (1) + .06	2 (2) ∅ .06
Top Mgt.	6 (7) -	2 (3) -	6 (4) +	2 (1) +	3 (1) +	.48	2 (0) +	2 (2) ∅	4 (3) +	1 (7) -
Board/Owner	1 (1) ∅ .03	0 (0) ∅ .00	0 (0) ∅ .00	0 (0) ∅ .00	0 (0) ∅ .00	2 (0) + .06	.06	0 (0) ∅ .00	0 (0) ∅ .00	0 (1) - .00

Function	Pur-chasing	Engin-eering	Mfg./Prod.	Acctg./Finance	Sales/Mktg.	Top Mgt.	Board/Owner	Maint. Services	Others	Vendors
Maint. Serv.	5 (4) + .16	3 (1) + .10	2 (2) ∅ .06	0 (1) - .00	1 (1) ∅ .03	2 (2) ∅ .06	0 (0) ∅ .00	.26	1 (2) - .03	1 (4) - .03
Others	9 (6) + .26	3 (2) + .10	3 (3) ∅ .10	0 (1) - .00	2 (1) + .06	4 (3) + .13	0 (0) ∅ .00	1 (2) - .03	.42	7 (7) ∅ .23
Vendors	25 (14) + .81	6 (5) + .19	5 (8) - .16	1 (2) - .03	2 (2) ∅ .06	1 (7) - .03	0 (1) - .00	1 (4) - .03	9 (7) + .29	1.0

TOTAL COMMUNICATION LINKS = 265

Main Diagonal Cells = % of involvement in 31 cases

Off Diagonal Cells =

Observed (Expected)
more/less
% of cases

Others.
 Inside--construction, requisition control, architect, inspection, office manager, lab manager, traffic manager, personnel, legal
 Outside--customer, advertising agency, testing lab, managers

182

REFERENCES

Aldrich, Howard, and Diane Herker. 1977. "Boundary Spanning Roles and Organizational Structure." Academy of Management Review 2 (April): 217-30.

Ammer, D. S. 1968. Materials Management. 2d ed. Homewood, Ill.: Richard D. Irwin.

_____. 1962. "Realistic Reciprocity." Harvard Business Review 40: 116-24.

Anyon, G. J. 1963. Managing an Integrated Purchasing Process. New York: Holt, Rinehart and Winston.

Arndt, Johan. 1967. "Role of Product-Related Conversations in the Diffusion of a New Product." Journal of Marketing Research 4 (August): 291-95.

Backhaus, K., and B. Gunter. 1976. "A Phase-Differentiated Interaction Approach to Industrial Marketing Decisions." Industrial Marketing Management 5: 255-70.

Bagozzi, R. P. 1975. "Marketing as Exchange." Journal of Marketing 39: 32-39.

Baker, Michael J. 1975. Marketing New Industrial Products. London: Macmillan Press.

Bales, R. F., and F. L. Strodtbeck. 1951. "Phases in Group Problem Solving." Journal of Abnormal and Social Psychology 46: 485-95.

Bartlett, M.S. 1950. "Tests of Significance in Factor Analysis." British Journal of Psychology (Statistical Section) 3: 77-85.

Bauer, R. A. 1960. "Consumer Behavior as Risk Taking." In Dynamic Marketing for a Changing World, edited by R. S. Hancock, pp. 389-98. Chicago: American Marketing Association.

Bavelas, A. 1950. "Communication Patterns in Task-Oriented Groups." Journal of Accoustical Society of America 22: 725-30.

Bearden, James H. 1967. "A Measure of the Occupational Status of Purchasing Agents." Journal of Purchasing 3 (May): 62-68.

Berlo, David K., et al. 1972. "An Analysis of the Communication Structure of the Office of Civil Defense." Unpublished report, Michigan State University.

Blau, Peter M. 1970. "A Formal Theory of Differentiation in Organizations." American Sociological Review 35 (April): 201-18.

Bonoma, T. V., R. Bagozzi, and G. Zaltman. 1978. "The Dyadic Paradigm with Specific Application toward Industrial Marketing." In Organizational Buying Behavior, edited by T. V. Bonoma and G. Zaltman, pp. 49-66. Chicago: American Marketing Association.

Bonoma, T. V., and W. J. Johnston. 1978. "The Social Psychology of Industrial Buying and Selling." Industrial Marketing Management 7: 62-84.

Bonoma, T. V., G. Zaltman, and W. J. Johnston. 1978. Industrial Buying Behavior. Marketing Science Institute Monograph. Cambridge, Mass.: Marketing Science Institute.

Brand, G. T. 1972. The Industrial Buying Decision. New York: Wiley.

Buckner, H. 1967. How British Industry Buys. London: Hutchinson.

Busch, P., and P. T. Wilson. 1976. "An Experimental Analysis of a Salesman's Expert and Referent Bases of Social Power in the Buyer-Seller Dyad." Journal of Marketing Research 13: 3-11.

Buzzell, R. D., et al. 1964. Marketing—A Contemporary Analysis. Homewood, Ill.: Richard D. Irwin, pp. 206-25.

Calder, B. J. 1977. "Structural Role Analysis of Organizational Buying: A Preliminary Investigation." In Consumer and Industrial Buying Behavior, edited by J. Sheth, A. Woodside, and P. Bennett, pp. 193-200. New York: Elsevier-North Holland.

Capon, Noel, and James Hulbert. 1975. "Decision Systems Analysis in Industrial Marketing." Industrial Marketing Management 4: 143-60.

Cardozo, R. N., and J. W. Cagley. 1971. "An Experimental Study of Industrial Buyer Behavior." Journal of Marketing Research 8 (August): 329-34.

Child, John. 1972. "Organization Structure and Strategies of Control: A Replication of the Aston Studies." Administrative Science Quarterly 17: 163-77.

Choffray, J. M. 1977. "A Methodology for Investigating the Nature of the Industrial Adoption Process and the Differences in Perceptions and Evaluation Criteria among Decision Participants." Unpublished Ph.D. dissertation, Massachusetts Institute of Technology.

Choffray, J. M., and G. Lilien. 1978. "Assessing Response to Industrial Marketing Strategy." Journal of Marketing 42: 20-31.

_____. 1976. "Models of the Multiperson Choice Process with Application to the Adoption of Industrial Products." Sloan School working paper no. 861-76, Massachusetts Institute of Technology (June).

Cooley, J. R., D. W. Jackson, and L. R. Ostrom. 1977. "Analyzing the Relative Power of Participants in Industrial Buying Decisions." In Contemporary Marketing Thought, edited by B. A. Greenberg and D. N. Bellenger, pp. 243-46. Chicago: American Marketing Association.

Cooley, J. R., and P. R. Lohnes. 1971. Multivariate Data Analysis. New York: John Wiley & Sons.

Corey, E. R. 1976. Industrial Marketing: Cases and Concepts. 2d ed. Englewood Cliffs, N.J.: Prentice-Hall.

Cox, D. F. 1967. "Risk Taking and Information Handling in Consumer Behavior." Division of Research, Graduate School of Business, Harvard University.

Cyert, R. M., and K. R. MacCrimmon. 1968. "Organizations." In The Handbook of Social Psychology, edited by G. Lindsey and E. Aronson, 2d ed., vol. 2, pp. 568-611. Reading, Mass.: Addison-Wesley.

Cyert, R. M., and J. G. March. 1963. A Behavioral Theory of the Firm. Englewood Cliffs, N.J.: Prentice-Hall.

Cyert, R. M., H. A. Simon, and D. B. Trow. 1956. "Observation of a Business Decision." Journal of Business 29 (October): 237-48.

Czepiel, J. A. 1974. "Word-of-Mouth Processes in the Diffusion of a Major Technological Innovation." Journal of Marketing Research 11 (May): 172-80.

Downs, George W., Jr., and Lawrence B. Mohr. 1972. "Conceptual Issues in the Study of Innovation." Administrative Science Quarterly 17: 163-77.

Driver, Michael J., and Siegfried Streufert. 1966. "Group Composition, Input Load and Group Information Process." Institute for Research in the Behavioral, Economic, and Management Science, Institute paper no. 142, Graduate School of Industrial Administration, Purdue University.

Duncan, D. J. 1966. "Purchasing Agents: Seekers of Status Personal and Professional." Journal of Purchasing 2: 17-26.

_____. 1940. "What Motivates Business Buyers." Harvard Business Review 17 (Summer): 448-54.

Evans, F. B. 1963. "Selling as a Dyadic Relationship—A New Approach." American Behavioral Scientist 6: 76-79.

Faris, C. W. 1967. "Market Segmentation and Industrial Buying Behavior." In Marketing for Tomorrow . . . Today, edited by M. S. Moyer and R. E. Vosburgh, pp. 108-10. Chicago: American Marketing Association.

Feldman, W., and R. Cardozo. 1969. "The Industrial Revolution and Models of Buyer Behavior." Journal of Purchasing 5: 77-88.

"Finding the Industrial Buying Influence." 1968. Marketing Insights, April 15, pp. 14-16.

French, J. R. P., Jr., and B. Raven. 1959. "The Bases of Social Power." In Studies in Social Power, edited by D. Cartwright, pp. 150-57. Ann Arbor, Mich.: Institute for Social Research.

Galbraith, J. 1977. Organization Design. Reading, Mass.: Addison-Wesley.

Glanzer, M., and R. Glaser. 1961. "Techniques for the Study of Group Structure and Behavior: II. Empirical Studies of the Effects of Structure in Small Groups." Psychological Bulletin 58: 1-27.

Gorman, Ronald H. 1971. "Role Conception and Purchasing Behavior." Journal of Purchasing 7 (February): 57-71.

Grashof, John F., and Gloria P. Thomas. 1976. "Industrial Buying Center Responsibilities: Self versus Other Member Evaluations of Importance." In Marketing: 1776-1976 and Beyond, edited by K. R. Bernhard, pp. 344-47. Chicago: American Marketing Association.

Green, P. E., and D. S. Tull. 1976. Research for Marketing Decisions, 3d ed. Englewood Cliffs, N.J.: Prentice-Hall.

Gronhaug, K. 1977. "Exploring a Complex Organizational Buying Decision." Industrial Marketing Management 6: 439-45.

_____. 1976. "Exploring Environmental Influences in Organizational Buying." Journal of Marketing Research 13 (August): 225-29.

_____. 1975a. "Autonomous vs. Joint Decisions in Organizational Buying." Industrial Marketing Management 4: 265-71.

_____. 1975b. "Search Behavior in Organizational Buying." Industrial Marketing Management 4: 15-23.

Gummesson, Evert. 1978. "Models of Organizational Buying Behavior, Their Relevance for Professional Service Marketing." Marketing for Public Agencies Organizational Buying Behavior, Proceedings of a research seminar. Senanque, France: Université d'Aix-Marseille.

Haas, R. 1976. Industrial Marketing Management. New York: Petrocelli/Charter.

Hage, Jerald, and Michael Aiken. 1970. Social Change in Complex Organizations. New York: Random House.

Hakansson, H., and C. Ostberg. 1955. "Industrial Marketing: An Organizational Problem?" Industrial Marketing Management 4: 113-23.

Hakansson, H., and B. Wootz. 1975. "Supplier Selection in an Industrial Environment—An Experimental Study." Journal of Marketing Research 12 (February): 46-51.

Harary, F., R. Z. Nouman, and D. Cartwright. 1958. Structural Models: An Introduction to the Theory of Directed Graphs. New York: John Wiley & Sons.

Harding, M. 1966. "Who Really Makes the Purchasing Decisions?" Industrial Marketing 51 (September): 76-81.

Harman, H. H. 1967. Modern Factor Analysis, 2d ed. Chicago: University of Chicago Press.

Heider, Fritz. 1958. The Psychology of Interpersonal Relations. New York: John Wiley & Sons.

Hill, R. M., R. S. Alexander, and J. S. Cross. 1975. Industrial Marketing, 4th ed. Homewood, Ill." Richard D. Irwin.

Hill, Roy W. 1973. Marketing Technological Products to Industry. Oxford, England: Pergamon Press.

Hillier, Terry J. 1975. "Decision-Making in the Corporate Industrial Buying Process." Industrial Marketing Management 4: 99-106.

_____. 1972. "Decision Making in the Industrial Buying Process." Unpublished Ph.D. dissertation, University of Bradford, England.

Hirsch, W. Z. 1960. "Decision Making in Industrial Marketing." Journal of Marketing 24 (January): 21-27.

Howard, John A. 1963a. Marketing: Executive and Buyer Behavior. New York: Columbia University Press.

_____. 1963b. Marketing Management: Analysis and Planning. Homewood, Ill.: Richard D. Irwin.

Howard, John A., and W. M. Morgenroth. 1968. "Information Processing Model of Executive Decision." Management Science 14 (March): 416-28.

Howard, John A., and J. N. Sheth. 1969. The Theory of Buyer Behavior. New York: John Wiley & Sons.

Jackson, John H., and Don Sciglimpaglia. 1974. "Toward a Role Model of the Organizational Purchasing Process." Journal of Purchasing and Materials Management 10 (May): 23-40.

Jacobson, E., and S. E. Seashore. 1951. "Communication Practices in Complex Organizations." Journal of Social Issues 7: 28-40.

James, B. G. S. 1967. "The Industrial Market Practices, Motives and Their Marketing Implications." European Journal of Marketing 1: 25-34.

Johnston, W. J., and T. V. Bonoma. 1978. "Prototypical Power Systems: A Social Psychological Approach to Industrial Marketing." In Research Frontiers in Marketing: Dialogues and Directions, edited by S. C. Jain, pp. 102-6. Chicago: American Marketing Association.

_____. 1977. "Reconceptualizing Industrial Buying Behavior: Toward Improved Research Approaches." In Contemporary Marketing Thought, edited by B. A. Greenberg and D. N. Bellenger, pp. 247-51. Chicago: American Marketing Association.

Katz, L. 1953. "A New Status Index Derived from Sociometric Analysis." Psychometrika 18: 39-43.

Keeney, Ralph L., and Howard Raiffa. 1976. Decisions with Multiple Objectives: Preference and Value Trade-Offs. New York: John Wiley & Sons.

Kernan, J. B., and M. S. Sommers. 1967. "Role Theory and Behavioral Style." Journal of Purchasing 3: 27-28.

_____. 1966. "The Behavioral Matrix: A Closer Look at the Industrial Buyer." Business Horizons 9: 59-72.

Kiser, G. E., C. P. Rao, and S. R. G. Rao. 1975. "Vendor Attribute Evaluations of Buying Center Members Other Than Purchasing Executives." Industrial Marketing Management 4: 45-54.

Kotler, Phillip. 1980. Marketing Management: Analysis, Planning and Control. 4th ed. Englewood Cliffs, N.J.: Prentice-Hall.

_____. 1976. Marketing Management: Analysis, Planning and Control. 2d ed. Englewood Cliffs, N.J.: Prentice-Hall.

Kuhn, Thomas S. 1970. The Structure of Scientific Revolutions. 2d ed. Chicago: University of Chicago Press.

Lambert, D. R., R. J. Dornoff, and J. B. Kernan. 1977. "The Industrial Buyer and the Postchoice Evaluation Process." Journal of Marketing Research 14 (May): 246-51.

Lancaster, G. A., and M. White. 1976. "Industrial Diffusion, Adoption, and Communication." European Journal of Marketing 10: 280-98.

Lazo, H. 1960. "Emotional Aspects of Industrial Buying." In Dynamic Marketing for a Changing World, edited by R. S. Hancock, pp. 258-65. Chicago: American Marketing Association.

Lehman, M. A., and R. M. Cardozo. 1973. "Product or Industrial Advertisements." Journal of Advertising Research, April, pp. 43-47.

Lehmann, Donald R., and John O'Shaughnessy. 1974. "Difference in Attribute Importance for Different Industrial Products." Journal of Marketing 38 (April): 36-42.

Levitt, T. 1967. "Communications and Industrial Selling." Journal of Marketing 31: 15-21.

Mansfield, Roger. 1973. "Bureaucracy and Centralization: An Examination of Organizational Structure." Administrative Science Quarterly 18: 477-88.

March, J. C., and H. A. Simon. 1958. Organizations. New York: John Wiley & Sons.

Martilla, J. A. 1971. "Word-of-Mouth Communication in the Industrial Adoption Process." Journal of Marketing Research, May, pp. 173-78.

Mathews, H. Lee., James Robeson, and P. J. Bambic. 1977. "Achieving Seller Acceptability in Industrial Markets: Development of the Communication Mix." In Consumer and Industrial Buying Behavior, edited by J. Sheth, A. Woodside, and P. Bennett, pp. 221-28. New York: Elsevier-North Holland.

McAleer, G. 1974a. "Buying Influence—A Verified Basis for Segmentation within an Industrial Market." Southern Marketing Association Proceedings, pp. 71-75.

_____. 1974b. "Do Industrial Advertisers Understand What Influences Their Markets?" Journal of Marketing 38: 15-23.

McMillan, James R. 1973. "Role Differentiation in Industrial Buying Decisions." In Conceptual and Methodological Foundations of Marketing, edited by T. V. Greer, pp. 207-11. Chicago: American Marketing Association.

Metaxas, T. 1962. Capital Goods Buying: Teamwork's Essential Purchasing, vol. 59, pp. 70-73.

Mogee, Mary Ellen, and Alden S. Bean. 1977. "The Role of the Purchasing Agent in Industrial Innovation." In Organizational Buying Behavior, edited by T. V. Bonoma and G. Zaltman, pp. 126-37. Chicago: American Marketing Association.

Monoky, J. F., Jr. 1973. "Pretences and Attitudes toward Sources of Information by Industrial Purchasing Agents as a Function of the Buying Situation." Unpublished Ph.D. dissertation, Pennsylvania State University.

Monoky, J. F., H. Lee Mathews, and D. T. Wilson. 1975. "Information Source Preference by Industrial Buyers as a Function of the Buying Situation." Working paper no. 27, College of Business Administration, Pennsylvania State University.

Moriarty, R. T., and M. Galper. 1978. "Organizational Buying Behavior: A State-of-the-Art Review and Conceptualization." Marketing Science Institute working paper, Report nos. 78-101, Cambridge, Mass., March.

Moyer, R. 1970. "Reciprocity: Retrospect and Prospect." Journal of Marketing 34: 47-54.

Nicosia, F., and Y. Wind. 1977. "Behavioral Models of Organization Buying Processes." In Behavioral Models for Market Analysis: Foundations of Marketing Action, edited by F. Nicosia and Y. Wind, pp. 96-120. Hinsdale, Ill.: Dryden Press.

Nie, N. H., C. H. Hull, J. G. Jenkins, K. Steinbrenner, and D. H. Bent. 1975. Statistical Package for the Social Sciences. New York: McGraw-Hill.

Ozanne, U. B., and G. A. Churchill. 1971. "Five Dimensions of the Industrial Adoption Process." Journal of Marketing Research, August, pp. 322-28.

Parket, R. 1973. "The Challenge from Industrial Buyer Perception of Product Non Differentiation." Industrial Marketing Management 2 (June): 281-88.

_____. 1972. "The Effects of Product Perception on Industrial Buyer Behavior." Industrial Marketing Management 1 (April): 339-46.

Patchen, M. 1975. "The Locus and Basis of Influence on Organizational Decisions." Organizational Behavior and Human Performance 11: 195-221.

_____. 1969. "Case Studies of Decision-Making in Organizations." Survey Research Center, Institute for Social Research, University of Michigan.

Perrow, Charles. 1967. "A Framework for the Comparative Analysis of Organizations." American Sociological Review 32 (April): 194-208.

Peters, M. P., and M. Venkatesan. 1973. "Exploration of Variables Inherent in Adopting an Industrial Product." Journal of Marketing Research 10: 312-15.

Pettigrew, A. M. 1975. "The Industrial Purchasing Decision as a Political Process." European Journal of Marketing 9: 4-19.

Purchasing Magazine Readers Have Something to Tell You about Chemicals, Report 10-A. 1965. New York: Purchasing Magazine, pp. 7-8.

Rijcke, J. C. de. 1978. "Perception of Self versus Others Role in Different Stages of a New Buy Situation: A Survey with Purchasing and Non Purchasing Executives." Marketing for Public Agencies Organizational Buying Behavior, Proceedings of a research seminar. Senanque, France: Université d'Aix-Marseille, pp. 252-63.

Risley, G. 1972. Modern Industrial Marketing: A Decision-Making Approach. New York: McGraw-Hill.

Robertson, Thomas S. 1971. Innovative Behavior and Communication. New York: Holt, Rinehart and Winston.

Robey, D., M. M. Bakr, and T. S. Miller. 1977. "Organizational Size and Management Autonomy: Some Structural Discontinuities." Academy of Management Journal 21: 378-97.

Robey, D., and W. J. Johnston. 1977. "Lateral Influences and Vertical Authority in Organizational Buying." Industrial Marketing Management 6: 451-62.

Robinson, P. J. 1968. "Some Alternative Approaches to Modeling and Evaluating Industrial Marketing Strategies." In A New Measure of Responsibility for Marketing, edited by K. Cox and D. M. Enis, pp. 273-83. Chicago: American Marketing Association.

Robinson, P. J., C. W. Faris, and Y. Wind. 1967. Industrial Buying and Creative Marketing. Boston: Allyn and Bacon.

Robinson, P. J., and B. Stidsen. 1967. Personal Selling in a Modern Perspective. Boston: Allyn and Bacon.

Rogers, E. M., and A. R. Rogers. 1976. Communication in Organizations. New York: Free Press.

Saleh, F. A., B. J. LaLonde, J. R. Rile, and J. R. Grabner. 1971. "Modeling Industrial Buyer Behavior: The Purchase of Motor Carrier Services." In Relevance in Marketing: Problems, Research, Action, edited by F. C. Allvine, pp. 402-10. Chicago: American Marketing Association.

Schroder, H., M. Driver, and S. Streufert. 1966. Human Information Processing. New York: Holt, Rinehart and Winston.

Schwartz, D. F., and E. Jacobson. 1977. "Organizational Communication Network Analysis: The Liaison Communication Role." Organizational Behavior and Human Performance 18: 158-74.

Scientific American. 1969. How Industry Buys—1970. New York: Scientific American.

_____. 1950. How Industry Buys. New York: Scientific American.

Scott, Jerome E., and Peter Wright. 1976. "Modeling an Organizational Buyer's Product-Evaluation Strategy: Validity and Pro-
cedural Consideration." Journal of Marketing Research 13
(August): 211-24.

Shaw, M. E. 1964. "Communication Networks." In Advances in
Experimental Social Psychology, edited by L. Berkowitz. New
York: Academic Press.

Shepherd, M., Jr. 1968. "Buyers Must Be More than Data Trans-
mitters." Purchasing Magazine, January 11, p. 61.

Sheth, J. N. 1977. "Recent Developments in Organizational Buying
Behavior." In Consumer and Industrial Buying Behavior,
edited by J. Sheth, A. Woodside, and P. Bennett, pp. 17-34.
New York: Elsevier-North Holland.

_____. 1973. "A Model of Industrial Buyer Behavior." Journal of
Marketing 37 (October): 50-56.

Spekman, R. 1978. "A Macro-Sociological Examination of the Industrial Buying Center: Promise or Problems?" In Research
Frontiers in Marketing: Dialogues and Directions, edited by
S. C. Jain, pp. 111-15. Chicago: American Marketing Association.

_____. 1977. "A Contingency Approach to Power Relationships
within the Organizational Buying Task Group." Unpublished
Ph.D. dissertation, Northwestern University.

Spekman, R., and G. T. Ford. 1977. "Perceptions of Uncertainty
within a Buying Group." Industrial Marketing Management 6:
395-403.

Stevens, J., and J. Grant. 1975. The Purchasing/Marketing Interface. New York: John Wiley & Sons.

Stiles, G. W. 1973. "An Information Processing Model of Industrial
Buyer Behavior. In Conceptual and Methodological Foundations
of Marketing, edited by T. V. Greer, pp. 534-35. Chicago:
American Marketing Association.

_____. 1972. "Determinants of the Industrial Buyer's Level of In-
formation Processing: Organizations, Situations and Individual
Differences." Paper presented at the Association for Consumer

Research/American Marketing Association workshop, University of Chicago.

Strauss, George. 1964. "Workflow Frictions, Interfunctional Rivalry, and Professionalism: A Case Study of Purchasing Agents." Human Organization 23 (Summer): 137-49.

_____. 1962. "Tactics of Lateral Relationship: The Purchasing Agent." Administrative Science Quarterly 7 (September): 161-86.

Sweeney, T. W., H. Lee Mathews, and D. T. Wilson. 1973. "An Analysis of Industrial Buyers' Risk Reducing Behavior: Some Personality Correlates." In Conceptual and Methodological Foundations of Marketing, edited by T. V. Greer, pp. 217-21. Chicago: American Marketing Association.

Thayer, L. 1967. "Communication and Organizational Theory." In Human Communication Theory, edited by F. E. X. Dance, pp. 70-115. New York: Holt, Rinehart and Winston.

Thomas, R., and Y. Wind. 1977. "On the Status of Organizational Buying Behavior." Working paper, University of Pennsylvania.

Tushman, M. L. 1977. "Special Boundary Roles in the Innovation Process." Administrative Science Quarterly 22 (December): 587-605.

Van de Water, J. 1961. "Centralize and Save." Purchasing 58: 89-93.

von Bertalanffy, Ludwig. 1968. General Systems Theory. New York: Braziller.

Vroom, V. H., and P. W. Yetton. 1973. Leadership and Decision-Making. Pittsburgh, Pa.: University of Pittsburgh Press.

Walsh, C. E. 1961. "Reaching Those 'Hidden' Buying Influences." Industrial Marketing, October, pp. 164-70.

Webster, F. E., Jr. 1970. "Informal Communication in Industrial Markets." Journal of Marketing Research 7 (May): 186-89.

_____. 1968a. "On the Applicability of Communication Theory to Industrial Markets." Journal of Marketing Research 5 (November): 426-28.

_____. 1968b. "Word-of-Mouth Communication and Opinion Leadership in Industrial Markets." In Marketing and the New Science of Planning, edited by R. L. King, pp. 455-59. Chicago: American Marketing Association.

_____. 1965. "Modeling the Industrial Buying Process." Journal of Marketing Research 2 (November): 370-76.

Webster, F. E., Jr., and Y. Wind. 1972a. "A General Model for Understanding Organizational Buying Behavior." Journal of Marketing 36 (April): 12-19.

_____. 1972b. Organizational Buying Behavior. Englewood Cliffs, N.J.: Prentice-Hall.

Weigand, Robert E. 1968. "Why Studying the Purchasing Agent Is Not Enough." Journal of Marketing 32 (January): 41-45.

_____. 1966. "Identifying Industrial Buying Responsibility." Journal of Marketing Research 3 (February): 81-84.

Wildt, A. R., and A. V. Bruno. 1974. "The Prediction of Preference for Capital Equipment Using Linear Attitude Models." Journal of Marketing Research 11 (May): 203-5.

Wilks, S. S. 1932. "Certain Generalizations in the Analysis of Variance." Biometrika 24: 471-74.

Wilson, D. T. 1971. "Industrial Buyer's Decision-Making Styles." Journal of Marketing Research 8 (November): 433-36.

Wilson, D. T., H. Lee Mathews, and T. V. Sweeney. 1971. "Industrial Buyer Segmentation: A Psychographic Approach." In Relevance in Marketing: Problems, Research, Action, edited by F. C. Allvine, pp. 327-31. Chicago: American Marketing Association.

Wind, Y. 1978. "Organizational Buying Behavior." In Review of Marketing, edited by G. Zaltman and T. V. Bonoma, pp. 160-93. Chicago: American Marketing Association.

_____. 1971. "A Reward Balance Model of Buying Behavior in Organizations." In New Essays in Marketing Theory, edited by G. Fisk, pp. 206-17. Boston: Allyn and Bacon.

_____. 1970. "Industrial Source Loyalty." Journal of Marketing Research 7 (November): 450-57.

_____. 1965. "Applying the Behavioral Theory of the Firm to Industrial Buying Decisions." Economic and Business Bulletin 20 (Spring): 22-28.

Wind, Y., and P. J. Robinson. 1968. "Simulating the Industrial Buying Process." In Marketing and the New Science of Planning, edited by R. L. King, pp. 441-48. Chicago: American Marketing Association.

Wind, Y., and F. E. Webster, Jr. 1972. "Industrial Buying as Organizational Behavior: A Guideline for Research Strategy." Journal of Purchasing 8 (August): 5-16.

Witt, Robert E., and G. D. Bruce. 1972. "Group Influence on Brand Choice Congruence." Journal of Marketing Research 9 (November): 440-43.

Yankelovich, D. 1964. "New Criteria for Market Segmentation." Harvard Business Review 42: 83-90.

Zaltman, G. 1975. "The Frontiers of Marketing." Albert W. Frey Lecture, University of Pittsburgh.

Zaltman, G., and T. V. Bonoma. 1977. "Organizational Buying Behavior: Hypotheses and Directions." Industrial Marketing Management 6: 53-60.

Zaltman, G., R. Duncan, and J. Holbek. 1973. Innovations and Organizations. New York: John Wiley Interscience.

ABOUT THE AUTHOR

WESLEY J. JOHNSTON is Assistant Professor of Marketing and Industrial Management at the College of Administrative Sciences, Ohio State University.

Dr. Johnston has written numerous journal articles dealing with the topics of industrial buying behavior, sales force management, and international marketing. In addition, he has coauthored a Marketing Science Institute monograph entitled Industrial Buying Behavior.

Dr. Johnston received his M.B.A. and Ph.D. degrees in business administration from the University of Pittsburgh.